BUSINESS MANAGEMENT
(A Brief Exposé)

by
Jacob W. Chikuhwa

authorHOUSE®

AuthorHouse™ LLC
1663 Liberty Drive
Bloomington, IN 47403
www.authorhouse.com
Phone: 1-800-839-8640

Published by AuthorHouse 9/11/2013

ISBN: 978-1-4918-1537-3 (sc)
ISBN: 978-1-4918-1535-9 (hc)
ISBN: 978-1-4918-1536-6 (e)

Library of Congress Control Number: 2013916229

BUSINESS MANAGEMENT
(A Brief Exposé)

by
Jacob W. Chikuhwa

Other books by the author

Zimbabwe: The Rise to Nationhood
Zimbabwe at the Crossroads
Zimbabwe: Beyond a School Certificate
Shona Proverbs and Parables
In Communication with the Deceased
A Handbook in Business Management

To my parents

Wilson — Katiro (c. 1879 – March 3, 1972)
Cecilia — Ngwaranyi (c. 1901 – Aug. 5, 1991)

Who defied traditional beliefs
By declining to kill Jacob (one of the twins)

ACKNOWLEDGEMENTS

The writing and completion of this book involved intensive consultations with coleagues and people in the acedemia and executive officers in both private and public corporations in Zimbabwe and in Europe and the USA. Those who had read my other book, "A Handbook in Business Management" encouraged me to write this brief exposé in business management. I want to express my gratitude and appreciation for the petience and time taken by all concerned for their co-operation.

I have used a number of sources, and have drawn particularly from publications in the Bibliography. I would like to give special thanks to the authors and compilers of the various books, yearbooks, journals and periodical surveys and reports which made my task easier.

As always, I am beholden to my family. Pastors Doug and Jodi Fondell have been a beacon of inspiration and support throughout the years they have been at the head of the Immanuel International Church in Stockholm. Among other material support, they have helped me with marketing and publicising of my work.

Finally, I want to thank members of staff at AuthorHouse for the sterling effort they have put in making the publication of this book a reality.

CONTENTS

INTRODUCTION

It should be admitted that business studies is closely associated with manpower management, business administration, accountancy, marketing, purchasing and supply, product control, business law and a host of other subjects.

I have chosen manpower development, accounting procedures and data processing with the intention and hope to attempt a middle-of-the-road analysis to include those overlapping developments in business studies.

Therefore, the purpose is to give the reader an insight into the way organisations emerge and grow, and the relationships between manpower management, financial control and management information systems (MIS). A concerted effort has been made to project how one area is an integral part of the other. For one to succeed in business operations, one has to have the basic knowledge in the three areas of specialisation covered.

In certain cases, business management coincides with the concept of efficiency in the private enterprise, i.e. minimum production costs for a certain output, maximum profit and such economic laws as the law of diminishing returns, the law of supply and demand and so on.

To many people, economics seems difficult, even obscure. The main reason for this impression turns out to be that the money or financial aspects of the matter tend to be confusing. The crucial economic aspects, however, are generally much easier to grasp if the "veil of money" is lifted and the problem is looked at in real terms.

A considerable part of economics and especially the analysis of business efficiency, is based on a so-called opportunity cost argument, i.e. on the value of the best alternative use of a given resource, be it an available commodity, skilled manpower, a piece of machinery, or an hour of work.

A simple organisation structure with, among other units, personnel, finance and transport, can be created and in turn generate situations that are socially efficient in the sense that further changes which benefit both the individual and the organisation are possible. The vital property is the strategy set to merge social and technological parameters selected for the projected organisation. Once the selection of the manpower to operate the acquired machinery is completed, an all-out effort should be started to further develop their skills to increase efficiency.

The financial assumptions behind the organisation and manpower recruited to run the organisation must be considered. It is shown that a lack of financial expertise and absence of phenomena such as proper accounting procedures, the ability to keep proper books of accounts, etc. may ruin a good business proposal. It is further shown that a management interested in efficiency and increasing returns in production can neutralise or eliminate financial pitfalls, thus helping a dynamic organisation achieve its objectives.

With an efficient data processing system, it is possible to adjust the situation before it goes out of hand. Moreover, management may be dissatisfied with the way the finances of the organisation behave even if they tend towards the desired state. There are recurring shortfalls in the form of short-term general material and manpower problems. Management information systems are therefore important for the purpose of adjusting income distribution and combating tendencies towards general organisation inefficiency. Given carefully structured data processing systems, a general method can be established for decision-making or policy-making in individual cases of manpower recruitment and development, investment projects, income distribution, etc. — a so-called cost-benefit analysis.

ORGANISATION AND MANPOWER MANAGEMENT

Manpower management is the process where by individuals or persons are organised to take part in the active running of a particular organisation or company or task, in which at the end of the task there are benefits for both the person involved in the task and the organisation. While manpower management is the actual utilisation of man in the pursuit of a particular goal or objective, there is emphasis that such individual does not stray away from the focus or said target.

Manpower management is also known as human resource management which means employing people, developing their resources, utilising and upgrading their skills. The process involved are managing, planning, organising, directing and controlling.

Organisation Structure

While in-the-flesh organisations tend to be more or less complex, in the abstract, they can be made to appear rather simple. It is, in fact, true that an organisation is nothing more than a collection of people grouped together around a technology which is operated to transform inputs from its environment into marketable goods or services. Organisations inseparably intertwine people and processes into what is currently referred to as a "sociotechnical" system. People in organisations operate the technology, they run the process. But they in turn, as part of the process, have much of their behaviour determined by the system they operate.

The concept of structure we are going to employ here refers to the way in which departments or units are arranged within a system, the linkages established among these, and the wages in which positions are arranged within them. First, management establishes and modifies structure by the way in which it groups tasks into units. It may, for example, pull together related tasks around a given product or stage in the process.

Secondly, management establishes structure by binding units or departments together with lines of authority, responsibility, communication and control. The choice made in each of these areas clearly affects the role and task of the manager. Each subordinate manager's role and behaviour are strongly affected by the manner in which his unit is tied to those with whom it must interact.

Organisation and Manpower Management

The way in which information flows between or among such units, the individuals within the organisation to whom these units report, the manner in which their outputs are evaluated, etc, all influence managerial behaviour. The manager is not entirely controlled by the structure in which he operates but he is at least constrained by it.

Organisation structures should not be regarded as static. Like organisms, they change according to the prevailing environment although care must be taken not to make radical changes that may lead to disruption in the production of goods and services.

Organisation Variables

When we discuss organisations, we frequently feel the need to differentiate among them or to group them together along certain dimensions. Several such dimensions have been used, among the more prominent of which are goals and objectives, technology and manpower.

We differentiate between product/service, or output. Important differences appear to exist between a steel firm and an educational institute (although in this age of the conglomerate such differences seem to be disappearing), and we imply that a substantial gap does or should exist between religious and brokerage houses though each may feel that it is engaged in the determining and disseminating of services.

Similarly, we differentiate among organisations according to their technology, or the methods they use to get things done. A housewife concerned about zoning regulations has a mental picture of the characteristics of light versus heavy industry, and most of us, from observation or imagination, can discuss such differences and some of their more dramatic implications — as, say, between an assembly plant and a research and development organisation.

Finally, we regularly refer to or distinguish between organisations in accordance with characteristics (specialisation) related to their manpower. We separate, and have feelings about, large and small organisations, and we differentiate impersonal, professional, nationally owned and operated firms from locally controlled ones, frequently stating or implying a value judgement as we do.

Starlight Goals and Objectives

Jacob W. Chikuhwa

The goals and objectives of organisations, in theory and in fact (though the fact is sometimes difficult to describe), result from interactions with the environment. In the public sector, the idealised process occurs as follows:
(a) society has a visible need,
(b) constituents demand that it be filled,
(c) legislators vote into existence an organisation to meet this need, i.e. by an Act of Parliament. Of course, examples can be pointed out where the process appears to have been reversed, or begun in the middle, but generally this procedure tends to hold. In the private sector, the process, though somewhat less visible, is similar.

It is logical to consider land and buildings as the first requirement for the establishment of Starlight. The term 'land' is used to describe all those natural resources over which man has power of disposal and which may be used to yield an income. It includes, therefore, farming and building land, forests, mineral deposits, fisheries, rivers, lakes — all those resources freely supplied by nature which man needs in producing the things he wants. The supply of building land has increasingly become limited. Economists have always emphasised this particular aspect of land and there is one very important application of the principle of fixed supply in the case of the site value of land, especially in urban areas. On the other hand, the cost of putting up buildings is dictated by the prevailing retail prices of construction materials.

Whatever his personal motives, the entrepreneur moves to provide a product or service which the public will purchase, with the purchase demonstrating a real or presumed need. This process is sanctioned directly by the granting of a corporate charter or business licence, and indirectly by our total economic-political system, which promotes privately controlled production of goods and services.

Directors/managers may find that their primary task is that of attempting to cope with changing environmental demands, adjusting organisational goals and objectives as rapidly as possible in order to keep them aligned with the wishes of powerful constituents. Of course, even where the organisation is large and powerful, it generally finds it difficult to influence or maintain control over the demands of its environment completely and/or indefinitely. The most prestigious firms and governmental agencies have proved vulnerable to private and public

Organisation and Manpower Management

muckrakers and pressure groups lie in wait to ambush the organisation's efforts to protect itself from environmental demands. There appears to be a growing consensus that the need for managerial skill in adjusting rapidly to, or controlling, environmental demands is becoming increasingly essential.

Starlight Technology

The technology of an organisation includes not only the visible machinery, tools and equipment used in turning out its product or service, but also the specific human skills, knowledge and procedures used to operate these devices.

We can imagine various sets of continua on which we might classify and differentiate technologies. For example, we might array them from those built around simple, multipurpose hand tools to those that are highly specialised and almost completely automated. Or we might focus on the input and output ends of the process and arrange technologies in terms of the variability of the materials feeding in the complexity or the diversity of the products or services coming out.

Considering that we have derived a meaningful classification scheme in Starlight, that captured and highlighted the key variables among different technologies, we should then examine the impact of each class of category on management — on its role, attitudes and behaviour. A manager, of course, is not controlled by the organisation's technology, but its characteristics (specialisation) restrict the range of alternatives open to him at any given moment. One of his key tasks is, of course, to operate a technology as effectively and as efficiently as possible, but an increasingly important requirement is that he be able to cope with change — to recognise the need for and to make adjustments in the technology to keep it aligned with organisational needs and environmental influences, and at the same time to adjust his own role and behaviour to match the changes in technology.

It should be noted that working and productive capital accumulation together makes up the dominant component in the demand for finance in most concerns and consequently has to be trimmed to available finance, which, in turn, is composed of expected internal financing and borrowing. The basic factors determining investment goods demand are to be found among the factors determining the services and production planned.

Jacob W. Chikuhwa

Whenever the investment plans are elaborate in terms of project specifications — which is always the case in budgeting and usually the case in long-term planning — each project should be identified with a plan to e.g. expand capacity at a particular production line at one particular location and with elaborate technical specifications attached. After approval of the investment plan, an appropriation precedes each commitment to start spending on capital account. The appropriations plan or procedure is a matter of regular occurrence each month or more often and is carried out at several stages in the organisation's hierarchy.

In general, the investment plan and the appropriations plan (budget) are two different things. The investment plan is a solution to the comprehensive plan when all relevant factors have been taken into account. It defines how large a portion of total funds, expected to be available, that is planned to be allocated on capital account. It cannot be determined until the financing side has been considered. The appropriations plan comes later and is designed to finalise the selection of individual projects within the so determined frame. It is final and means authority to start making commitments. Normally, however, some individual project specification takes place already in the making of the investment plan.

Starlight Manpower

Manpower resources comprise the total effective effort that can be put to work as shown by the number of people and hours of work available, the capacity of employees to the work and their productivity.

After having classified employees by function and/or department, occupation, level of skill and status planned, it is management's task to select the people required. Besides the skills or abilities, from the point of view of the preparation of management development programmes, it can be equally important to select people with potential for advancement. Selection of manpower by age helps to pre-empt problems arising from a sudden rush of retirements or a preponderance of older employees. Another factor which is equally important is the length of service with previous employers for this will provide evidence of survival rates, which are a necessary tool for use by management in predicting future resources.

When selecting manpower, management considers manpower productivity and costs to be significant. Manpower selection is just as concerned with getting the numbers required as making the best use of the people selected. Selection methods should be designed with an objective to employ people with high performance potential and those with greater scope for personal achievement and recognition, more challenging and responsible work; people with more opportunity for individual advancement and growth at the same time as the new Starlight concern grows.

Once manpower has been selected and employed, it is important that management should put an effort into their development. This is concerned with improving the performance of employees, giving them opportunity for growth and development, and ensuring, so far as possible, that promotion within the organisation is provided for. The objectives of a typical manpower development programme can be defined as an endeavour to improve the financial and long-term growth of the organisation by:

(a) improving the performance of employees by seeing that they are clearly informed of their responsibilities and by agreeing with them specific key objectives against which their performance will be regularly assessed.

(b) identifying employees with further potential and ensuring that they receive the required development, training and experience to equip them for more senior posts within their own locations and divisions with the organisation.

The Role of Management and that of the Organisation

Setting up of a business concern does not end with the acquisition of land and buildings, plant and equipment and the recruitment of personnel to operate the technology. Immediately after setting up a business concern, the daunting process of development starts. It should be noted that development is an on-going process. Many an organisation have often grown from virtually back-yard and unknown concerns into giant conglomerates. One of the chief catalysts in the development of an organisation is management. The manager's chief task is that of integrating organisational and human variables into an effective and efficient sociotechnical system. On occasion, management carries out this task rationally and before the fact, attempting to blend an appropriate mix

Jacob W. Chikuhwa

of these variables. More often, management finds that someone has already provided them with a recipe and that one of the sets of variables, organisational or human, is more or less fixed and they must adjust the other set to it. Typical here is the situation where goals and objectives and technology are set and the manager's task is that of fitting persons with an appropriate set of characteristics to them. On occasion, however, the opposite occurs — the manager has before him a group of people with given characteristics (specialisations) for whom he must design appropriate objectives and a structure through which these can be accomplished.

Most often, the manager finds himself in the midst of an on-going sociotechnical system, with concurrent — and frequently conflicting — requirements for adjustments of both organisational and human needs and characteristics. The manager is influenced and/or constrained by both organisational and human variables and, in turn, as having an impact on them, modifying and adjusting them in the interest of organisational performance.

Just like a technician or mechanic, the manager uses certain tools — integrative tools or a set of mechanisms. The following mechanisms are some of the more important means by which managers carry out their integrative task:

(i) Direction

The manager attempts to blend human attitudes and energies to achieve organisational objectives through the mechanism of direction, i. e. decision and policy making, supervision, etc. He explains these objectives, plans how they can be attained, issues instructions concerning how, when, and by who these plans will be carried out, and, in person or through reports, oversees their progress. With regard to this mechanism, managerial behaviour might range:

(a) from unilateral determination of plans, policies and objectives to joint determination with those individuals affected;

(b) from close and direct supervision (either in person or through detailed procedures and reports) to general, supportive supervision which allows broad self-direction and self-control to be exercised in the pursuit of agreed-upon objectives.

(ii) Organisation and Job Design

Organisation and Manpower Management

Here the manager attempts to merge people and technology into a smooth functioning system by structuring and restructuring organisational units and the jobs which make up these units. Alternatives available in utilising these mechanisms might range:

(a) from structures which arrange groups of functional specialists in traditional hierarchical layers to more loosely linked, self-paced teams with heterogeneous skills grouped around a product, part, service, or integrated stage of the process;

(b) from job designs emphasising highly specialised and segmented collection of tasks to designs which attempt to encompass a meaningful range of activities into self-paced, self-evaluated operations.

(iii) Selection and Training — Appraisal and Development

On an on-going basis, the manager uses selection and training devices to find and hire people with characteristics appropriate to organisational needs, and, once the individuals are in the organisation, he uses appraisal and development mechanisms to maintain and enhance these characteristics. For these mechanisms, alternatives might range:

(a) from selection and training processes which focus on presumed traits and abilities associated with immediate job requirements to more flexible systems which attempt to balance the long-term needs of the organisation and the individual;

(b) from superior-conducted appraisal based on standard characteristics and behaviour to joint appraisal (superior/subordinates) focused on progress toward previously agreed upon job targets or objectives.

(c) from unilaterally planned and directed development programs to flexible procedures where organisation members are included in the process of setting their own development goals and choosing the means of achieving them.

(iv) Communication and Control

The manager builds linkages between the technical system and its human element and between segments of the sociotechnical system through communication and control systems. Here alternatives might range:

(a) from communication systems which primarily provide for downward flows of orders and instructions and upward flows of reports to

Jacob W. Chikuhwa

information systems designed to provide operating units with access to all the data they feel are necessary to their performance;

(b) control systems which collect progress information from operating units for transmission to distant evaluation points to short feedback loop designs which allow operating units to immediately appraise and adjust their own performance.

(v) Reward System

Finally, the manager uses a reward system to attract individuals to the organisation, maintain them within the system, and, hopefully, increase their performance level and contribution to the organisation. Within reward systems, alternatives might range:

(a) from systems built exclusively around either longevity or merit alone to more flexible systems which acknowledge both loyalty and performance;

(b) from unilateral determination of rewards and the method of their attainment to systems in which organisation members have a voice in determining the nature of rewards and the paths by which these can be achieved.

It should be acknowledged that while we have listed and described these mechanisms separately, they are in fact and in practice closely intertwined. They are all in operation, manifestly or latently, at the same time and what the manager does with regard to one of them affects what can and will be done with another. Unfortunately, many managers behave as if these mechanisms were separate and distinct and therefore fail, apparently, to recognise that what the one hand is accomplishing with adjustments to one mechanism, the other hand may be undoing with its adjustments to another.

It should not be overlooked that while managers are engaged in the activities to blend human attitudes and energies together with the organisation technology to achieve organisational objectives, they themselves need development. The traditional view is that the organisation need not concern itself with management development. The natural process of selection and the pressure of competition will ensure the survival of the fittest.

On the other hand, management development is seen mainly as a mechanical process using management inventories, multicoloured replacement charts, 'Cook's Tours' for newly recruited graduates, detailed job rotation programs, elaborate points schemes to appraise personal characteristics, and endless series of formal courses.

The true role of the organisation in management development lies somewhere between these two extremes. On the one hand it is not enough, in conditions of rapid growth (when they exist) and change, to leave everything to chance — to trial and error. On the other hand, elaborate management development programs cannot successfully be imposed on the organisation. Because development is always self-development, nothing could be more absurd than for the enterprise to assume responsibility for the development of a man. The responsibility rests with the individual, his abilities, his efforts and his creative foresight. Every manager in business has the opportunity to encourage individual self-development or to stifle it, to direct it or to misdirect it. He should be specifically assigned the responsibility for helping all men working with him to focus, direct and apply their self-development efforts productively. And every company can provide systematic development challenges to its managers.

Executive ability is eventually something which the individual must develop for himself on the job. But he will do this better if he is given encouragement, guidance and opportunities by his company and his manager. The role of the company is to provide conditions favourable to faster growth. And these conditions are very much part of the environment and organisation climate of the company and the management style of the chief executive who has the ultimate responsibility for management development.

Management development is not a separate activity to be handed over to a specialist and forgotten or ignored. The success of a management development program depends upon the degree to which all levels of management are committed to it. The development of subordinates must be recognised as a natural and essential part of any manager's job. But the lead must come from the top.

Management Development Activities

The management development activities required will depend on the organisation, on the one hand, its goals, its technology, its structure and philosophy and on the other hand, its human resources capabilities,

Jacob W. Chikuhwa

Fig. 1: Integration of Human and Organisational Variables

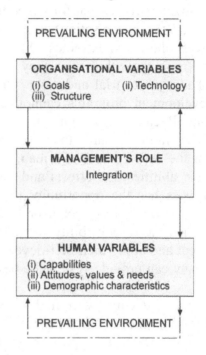

attitudes, values and needs and demographic characteristics (see Fig. 1). A bureaucratic, mechanistic type of organisation, such as a large government department, a nationalised industry, a major insurance firm or a large process manufacturing company, will be inclined to adopt the programmed routine approach, complete with a wide range of courses, inventories, replacement charts, career plans and management-by-objectives based review systems. An innovative and organic type of organisation may rightly dispense with all these mechanisms. Its approach should be to provide its managers with the opportunities, challenge and guidance they require, relying mainly on seizing the chance to give people extra responsibilities, and ensuring that they receive the coaching and encouragement they need. There may be no replacement charts, inventories or formal appraisal schemes, but people know how they stand, where they can go and how to get there.

Management development activities can be divided into seven areas:
(i)   Organisation Review
(ii)   Manpower Review

Fig. 2: The Process of Management Development

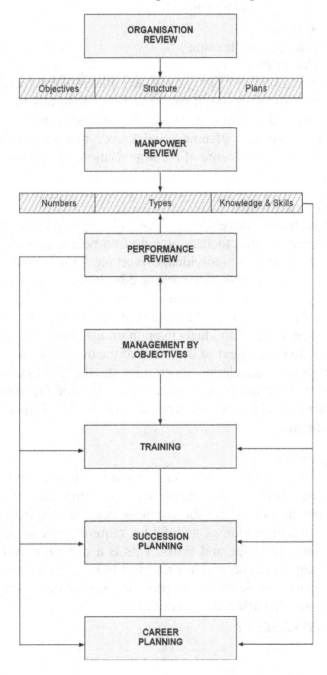

Jacob W. Chikuhwa

(iii)   Performance Review
(iv)   Management by Objectives
(v)   Training
(vi)   Succession Planning
(vii)   Career Planning

These manpower development activities are interrelated, as shown in Fig. 2, and, in this sense, it would be possible to talk about a 'program' of management development where the process consists of education and training, succession planning and career planning activities which are derived from the outcome of the organisation, manpower and performance reviews.

Organisation Review

Management development is closely related to organisation development, which focuses attention on people and the social system in which they work— individuals, working groups and the relationships between them — and uses various educational activities which may aim primarily to develop teamwork but also provide training for the individuals concerned. Management development appears to focus attention more on individuals than on groups and relationships, but it must do this with the context of the needs of the organisation as a whole.

Management development activities should therefore be founded upon a review of the objectives, structure and plans of the organisation and the implications of present weaknesses and future demands on managerial requirements.

Manpower Review

The organisation review leads naturally into a review of manpower resources. This is the manpower planning aspect of management development and, where the circumstances permit, it implies an analysis of the present resources and future requirements in terms of numbers, types and knowledge and skills. This is a general review, and individual and management succession needs would be analysed separately, although performance reviews will provide information on strengths and weaknesses that affect the overall plan.

Performance Review

Organisation and Manpower Management

Performance review systems are used to identify development needs by highlighting strengths and weaknesses and, so far as this is possible, potential for promotion. They are also a basis for the counselling and coaching activities which should form the most important part of an individual's development within the company. Performance review is a systematic method of obtaining, analysing and coding information about a person that is needed:

(a) for the better running of the business;

(b) by the manager to help him to improve the job holder's performance and plan his career;

(c) by the job holder to assist him to evaluate his own performance and develop himself.

There are three main groups of performance review activities:

(i)   Performance Reviews which relate to the need to improve the performance of individuals and thereby to improve the effectiveness of the organisation as a whole. The purpose is to analyse what a person has done and is doing in his job in order to help him to do better, by developing his strengths or by overcoming his weaknesses.

(ii) Potential Reviews which attempt to deal with the problem of predicting the level and type of work that the individual will be capable of doing in the future. This requires the analysis of existing skills, qualities and how they can be developed to the mutual advantage of the company and the employee, as well as the identification of any weaknesses which must be overcome if the employee's full potential is to be achieved. There is also an important counselling aspect to the review of potential which consists of discussions with the individual about his aspirations and how these can best be matched to the future foreseen for him.

(iii) Reward Reviews which relate to the distribution of such rewards as pay, power and status. In any company where rewards such as salary increments or bonuses are related to performance, there has to be some method of linking the two together. In some procedures, the rate of progression through a salary bracket or the size of the increment is derived from an overall assessment of performance, so that a top 'A' rating may

Jacob W. Chikuhwa

> result in a 10% merit increment while a middling 'C' rating
> may result in an average increment of 5%, or whatever
> inflationary conditions, the financial position of the company
> and current pay regulations allow.

Management by Objectives

Management by objectives is essentially a method of managing
organisations and people and of improving the performance of managers
who should, in turn, strive to improve the performance of their
subordinates. This is a dynamic system which aspires to integrate the
company's goals, technology and structure to achieve its profit and growth
with the manager's and subordinate's need to contribute and develop
themselves. The basic processes are:

(a) Subordinates agree with their managers the objectives of their job —
    expressed as targets or standards of performance for each key result
    area. The individual objectives are in line with unit and organisational
    objectives and are defined in a way which emphasises the contribution
    they make to achieving departmental and corporate plans.
(b) Performance is reviewed jointly by the manager and the subordinate to
    compare results with the defined objectives and standards.
(c) The manager and subordinates agree where improvements are required
    and how better results can be achieved and, as necessary, re-define
    targets and standards.

In behavioural science terms, 'An effective management must direct the
vision and efforts of all managers towards a common goal. It must ensure
that the individual manager understands what results are demanded of
him. It must ensure that the superior understands what to expect of each of
his subordinate managers. It must motivate each manager to maximum
efforts in the right direction. And while encouraging high standards of
workmanship, it must make them the means to the end of business
performance rather than the ends in themselves.'

Management by objectives is most effective when managers recognise
for themselves — with or without encouragement — that it is something
they can use to their own advantage. It is even more effective if they are
allowed the maximum amount of freedom to apply it in their departments
in their own way — let them develop their own forms, if they want to use
them. If not, let them do without. The agreed objectives can be written out

on a loose piece of paper if they prefer it that way — as long as they can find the piece of paper when it comes to a review.

Training

Management development is sometimes seen as primarily a matter of providing a series of appropriate courses at various points in a manager's career. But the best definition of training is the modification of behaviour through experience, which means that managers will develop best if they receive their training in the 'real' guided self-analysis.

The principal method by which managers can be equipped is by ensuring that they have the right variety of experience, in good time, in the course of their careers. This experience can and should be supplemented, but never replaced, by courses carefully timed and designed to meet particular needs.

It is necessary to state that while training is an important part of management development, it should not be allowed to degenerate into no more than a series of formal courses, even when these are based on elaborate job descriptions, job analyses and performance review systems. This guarantees a static and increasingly irrelevant approach. Formal training courses should only be used when it is essential to supplement what managers are learning on the job.

The key management development activity is therefore ensuring that managers are given the chance to learn; and this is primarily a matter of encouraging and stimulating on the job training and providing career opportunities to broaden experience.

The training techniques may be classified into three groups according to where they are generally used:

(a) On the job techniques — demonstration, coaching, job rotation/ planned experience.

(i) Demonstration is the technique of telling or showing a trainee how to do a job and then allowing him to get on with it. It is the most commonly used training method.

(ii) Coaching is a personal on the job training technique designed to develop individual skills, knowledge and attitudes. The term is usually reserved for management or supervisory training where informal, but planned encounters take place between managers and subordinates.

Jacob W. Chikuhwa

(iii) Finally, job rotation/planned experience aims to broaden experience by moving people from job to job or department to department. It can be an inefficient and frustrating method of acquiring additional knowledge and skills unless it is carefully planned and controlled. What has sometimes been referred to as the 'Cook's Tour' method of moving trainees (usually management trainees) from department to department has incurred much justified criticism because of the time wasted by trainees in departments where no one knew what to do with them or cared.

(b) On the job or off the job techniques — job (skill) instruction, question and answer assignments, projects, guided reading.

(i) Job (skill) instruction techniques should be based on skills analysis and learning theory. The sequence of instruction should follow four stages: 1) preparation, 2) presentation — explanation and demonstration and demonstration, 3) practice and testing and 4) follow-up.

(ii) The question and answer technique consists of an exchange between trainer and trainees to test understanding, stimulate thought or extend learning. It may take place during a job instruction programme or as a discussion period on a formal management course.

(iii) Assignments are a specific task or investigation which an individual does at the request of his trainer or manager.

(iv) Projects are broader studies or tasks which trainees are asked to complete, often with only very generalised guidelines from their trainer or manager. They encourage initiative in seeking and analysing information, in originating ideas and in preparing and presenting the results of the project.

(v) Lastly, knowledge can be increased by giving trainees books, handouts or company literature and asking them to read and comment on them.

(c) Off the job techniques — lecture, talk, discussion, 'discovery' method, case study, role playing, group exercise, group dynamics (team building), business game, programmed learning.

(i) A lecture is a talk with little or no participation except a question and answer session at the end. It is used to transfer information to an audience with controlled content and timing.

(ii) A talk is a less formal lecture for a smaller group of not more than 20 people which gives plenty of time for discussion.

(iii) The objectives of using discussion techniques are 1) get the audience to participate actively in learning; 2) give people an opportunity of learning from the experience of others; 3) help people to gain understanding of other points of view; and 4) develop powers of self-expression.

(iv) The discovery method is a style of teaching that allows the trainee to learn by finding out principles and relationships for himself. The essence of the method is that the training designer thinks out the progression of problems which the trainee is required to solve, relate this progression to the capacity of the trainee, and ensures that learning is based on intrinsic factors. In other words, the trainee does not need to rely on previous knowledge and experience, nor does he depend on outside assistance (i.e. extrinsic factors).

(v) A case study is a history or description of an event or set of circumstances which is analysed by trainees in order to diagnose the causes of a problem and work out how to solve it.

(vi) In role playing, the participants act out a situation by assuming the roles of the characters involved. The situation will be one in which there is interaction between two people within a group.

(vii) In a group exercise, the trainees examine problems and develop solutions to them as a group. The problem may be a case study or it could be a problem entirely unrelated to everyday work.

(viii) Group dynamics has three interconnected and often overlapping aims: 1) to improve the effectiveness with which groups operate (team building); 2) to increase self-understanding and awareness of social processes and 3) to develop interactive skills which will enable people to function more effectively in groups. Group training can also help in modifying individual attitudes and values.

(ix) A business game is an educational tool to test and develop a trainee's management skills and business knowledge. Players can see if they have what it takes to climb the corporate ladder, all the way to the top job. A trainee should correctly answer some (10 to 20) business-related multiple-choice questions in the allocated time and successfully climb some 8 levels of the corporate ladder — all the way to the top CEO job! When trainees play the game, their score is posted

Jacob W. Chikuhwa

to the Leader Board and, thus, can discover where they are ranked on the Leader Board. Have they achieved the highest salary at CEO level? (x) Programmed learning consists of a text which progressively feeds information to trainees. After each piece of information, questions are posed which the trainee should answer correctly before moving on.

Succession Planning

The aim of management succession planning is to ensure that as far as possible suitable managers are available to fill vacancies created by promotion, retirement, death, leaving or transfer. It also aims to ensure that a cadre of managers is available to fill the new appointments that may be established in the future.

The information for management succession planning comes from organisation and manpower reviews and assessments of performance and potential. This information needs to be recorded so that decisions can be made on promotions and replacements, and training or additional experience arranged for those with potential or who are earmarked for promotion.

Career planning

Career planning has two aims: first, to ensure that men and women of promise are given a sequence of experience that will equip them for whatever level of responsibility they have the ability to reach; secondly, to provide individuals with potential with the guidance and encouragement they may need if they are to fulfil their potential and remain with the organisation.

Career planning is most effective when it is linked to management succession planning so that the experience and training provided is leading towards a job that has to be filled. The extent to which careers can be planned, however, is limited if it is difficult to forecast replacement needs, assess long-term potential or provide an appropriate sequence of experience. These difficulties exist in most organisations and it is usually only possible to plan the next step towards promotion. But even that is better than leaving everything to chance.

Career planning may involve counselling individuals on their possible career paths and what they must do to achieve promotion. This does not mean that a long-range plan consisting of a number of predetermined steps

Organisation and Manpower Management

can be revealed. It is seldom, if ever, possible to be precise about long-term career prospects. Even if it were possible, it would be dangerous either to raise expectations which might not be fulfilled or to induce a feeling of complacency about the future. It may be feasible to talk about the next step, but beyond that, the wisest approach is to do no more than provide — in planning jargon — a scenario of the opportunities that might become available.

Career counselling should not be concerned with making what might turn out to be empty promises. Its main aim should be to help the individual concerned to help himself/herself by giving him/her some idea of the direction in which he/she ought to be heading.

FINANCIAL CONTROL

Financial control is defined as keeping costs to an agreed level, ensuring that a project is developed within budget. Critically, all managers should take responsibility for financial management and should not assume that this falls within the remit of the accounts team alone. Strategic or long-term planning is also a critical building block for effective financial control. This planning can help you to decide where your financial priorities lie and how much of your total budget can be allocated to different areas of the company or project.

Organisation/Business Objectives

Whether running or setting up a business, getting a first taste of responsibility accounts or taking a business course, the first steps towards an understanding of finance are the most difficult. The consequences of failing to understand business finance are not the same for everyone. The student simply fails an exam, while the businessman all too often loses his business, and the executive gets fired. Competition is generally greater today and the margin for mistakes smaller. The largest number of failures is in the early years, and the single most common cause is poor financial control.

People running small businesses frequently leave financial questions to their accountants to sort out at the year end. They often have the mistaken belief that keeping the books is an activity quite divorced from the 'real' task of getting customers or making products.

By the time the first set of figures is prepared, most small businesses are already too far down the road to financial failure to be saved. The final accounts become all too final and a good business proposition has been ruined by financial illiteracy. The few businessmen who do ask the way, perhaps of an accountant or bank manager, often do not understand the terms being used to explain the situation.

An understanding of financial reports is essential to anyone who wants to control a business, but simply knowing how these reports are constructed is not enough. To be effective, the businessman must be able to analyse and interpret that financial information.

It is highly likely that a business will want to borrow money either to get started or expand. Bankers and other sources of finance will use

Financial Control

specialised techniques to help them decide whether or not to invest. These techniques are the same as those used by the prudent businessman.

The starting point for any useful analysis is some appreciation of what should be happening in a given situation. All businesses have two fundamental objectives in common which allow us to see how well (or otherwise) they are doing:

(a) making a satisfactory return on investment and
(b) maintaining a sound financial position.

Making a Satisfactory Return on Investment

One of the main reasons for starting a business is to make a satisfactory return on investment (profit) on the money invested. One of the well known returns on investment is the building society deposit rate. In recent years, this has ranged between six and 12%, so for every $1,000 invested, depositors received between $60 and $120 return, each year. Their capital, in this example $1,000, remained intact and secure. To be 'satisfactory', the return must meet four criteria:

(i)   It must give a fair return to shareholders bearing in mind the risk they are taking. If the venture is highly speculative and the profits are less than the building society interest rates, your shareholders (yourself included) will not be happy.

(ii)   You must make enough profit to allow the company to grow. If a business wants to expand sales, it will need more working capital and eventually more space or equipment. The fastest and surest source of money for this is internally generated profits, retained in the business — reserves. It is indicated in the Balance Sheet that a business has three sources of new money: share capital or the owner's money; loan capital, put up by banks etc.; retained profits, generated by the business.

(iii)   The return must be good enough to attract new investors or lenders. If investors can get a greater return on their money in some other comparable business, then that is where they will put it.

(iv)   The return must provide enough reserves to keep the real capital intact. This means that you must recognise the impact inflation has on the business. A business retaining enough

Jacob W. Chikuhwa

profits each year to meet 5% growth in assets is actually contracting by 5% if inflation is running at 10%.

Table 1: Profit and Loss Account for Years 1 and 2

ITEM	$	$	%	$	$	%
SALES		100 000	100,0		130 000	100,0
Cost of Sales						
Materials	30 000		30,0	43 000		33,0
Labour	20 000	50 000	20,0	25 000	68 000	19,0
Gross Profit		50 000	50,0		62 000	48,0
EXPENSES						
Rent, Rates, etc.	18 000			20 000		
Wages	12 000			13 000		
Advertising	3 000			3 000		
Total Expenses	-	33 000		2 000	38 000	
Operating or Trading Profit		17 000	17,0		24 000	18,5
Deduct Interest on:						
Overdraft	900			800		
Loan	1 250	2 150		1 250	2 050	
Net Profit before Tax		14 850	14,8		21 950	16,8
Tax Paid		5 940			8 750	
Net Profit after Tax		8 910	8,9		13 200	10,1

There are a number of ways in which return on capital employed (ROCE) can be measured, but for a small business, two are particularly important. The ROCE is calculated by expressing the profit before long-term loan interest and tax as a proportion of the total capital employed. Thus, if you look at Starlight Profit and Loss Account (see Table 1), you can see that for year 1, the profit before tax is $14,850. To this, we have to add the loan interest of $1,250. If we did not do this, we would be double counting our cost of loan capital by expecting a return on a loan which had already paid interest. This makes the profit figure $16,100. We also ignore tax charges, not because they are unimportant or insignificant, but simply because the level of tax is largely outside the control of the business and it is the business's performance we are trying to measure.

Table 2: Balance Sheet for Year Ends 1 and 2

ITEM	$	$	$	$	$	$
FIXED ASSETS						
Furniture & Fixtures			12 500			28 110
WORKING CAPITAL						
Current Assets						
Stock	10 000			12 000		
Debtors	13 000			13 000		
Cash	100	23 100		500	25 500	
Less Current Liabilities						
Overdraft	5 000			6 000		
Creditors	1 690	6 690		5 500	11 500	
Net Current Assets			16 410			14 000
Capital Employed			28 910			42 110
FINANCED BY:						
Owner's Capital	10 000			18 910		
Profit Retained	8 910		18 910	13 200		32 110
Long-term Loan			10 000			10 000
TOTAL			28 910			42 110

Now look at the Balance Sheet in Table 2. The capital employed is the sum of the owner's capital, the profit retained and the long-term loan, in

Jacob W. Chikuhwa

this case $28,910 ($10,000 + $8,910 + $10,000). Thus, the ROCE ratio for the first year is:

$$\frac{\$16,100}{\$28,910} = 0.56 \text{ which expressed as a percentage} = 56\%$$

The great strength of this ratio lies in the overall view it takes of the financial health of the whole business. If you look at the same ratio for the second year, you will see a small change. The ratio gives no clue as to why this has happened — it simply provides the starting point for an analysis of business performance, and an overall yardstick with which to compare absolute performance.

The second way a small business would calculate a return on capital is by looking at the profit available for shareholders — return on shareholders' capital (ROSC). This is not the money actually paid out, for example, as dividends, but is a measure of increase in 'worth' of the funds invested by shareholders.

In this case, the net profit after tax is divided by the owner's capital plus the retained profits (these although not distributed, belong to the shareholders). Thus, in our example this would be the sum:

$$\frac{\$8,910}{\$18,910} = 0.47 \text{ which expressed as a percentage} = 47\%$$

And for the second year this ratio would be 41%.

Maintaining a Sound Financial Position

As well as making a satisfactory return, investors, creditors and employees expect the business to be protected from unnecessary risks. Clearly, all businesses are exposed to market risks: competitors, new products and price changes are all part of a healthy commercial environment. The sort of unnecessary risks that investors and lenders are particularly concerned about are high financial risks.

Cash flow problems are not the only threat to a business's financial position. Heavy borrowings can bring a high interest burden to a small business. This may be acceptable when sales and profits are good, and when times are bad, shareholders can be asked to tighten their belts. Bankers, however, expect to be paid all the time. Thus, business analysis and control are not just about profitability, but about survival and the practice of sound financial discipline.

All analysis of financial information requires comparisons. First, you can see how well you are meeting a personal goal. For example, you may want to double sales or add 25% to profits. In a more formalised business, this activity would be called budgeting, then comparisons would be made between actual results and the budget.

Second, you might want to see how well you are doing this year compared with last, or this month as opposed to the last, comparing performance against an historical standard. This is the way in which growth in sales or profits is often measured.

Thirdly, you may want to see how you are doing compared with someone else's business, perhaps a competitor, or someone in a similar line of business elsewhere. This may provide useful pointers to where improvements can be made, or to new and more profitable opportunities.

Budgeting for a Business

Everyone has made a budget or plan at some time. In our personal lives, we are always trying to match the scarce resource 'pay' with the ever expanding range of necessities and luxuries in the market place, a battle we all too often lose, with mortgage costs, or running expenses, food and children's clothes taking more cash out than we put in.

Temporary shortages of cash are made up by taking out an overdraft, the judicious use of a credit card, or talking to a rich aunt.

A business has to do much the same type of budgeting and planning, although much more thoroughly if it wants to survive and prosper. Some small businesses start off with their plans in the owner's head or on the back of the proverbial envelope. Most of these businesses end up going broke in the first year.

The central problem is that to make a profit, a business must take risks. A small new business must take many more risks than an established or larger one, with each risk having more important consequences if things go wrong.

Successful entrepreneurship is all about anticipating the sort of risks that have to be taken, and understanding how they will affect the business. Putting this information together usually means gathering facts and

Jacob W. Chikuhwa

opinions on the market place; interpreting their probable impact on your business; deciding what you want to happen; and finally deciding how you intend to make things happen; in other words, developing your strategy.

For a start, the plan or budget acts as a means of communicating your intentions to four vitally important audiences: the entrepreneur, the staff, shareholders and the providers of finance. You can experiment with various sales levels, profit margins and growth rates to arrive at a realistic picture of how you would like your business to develop, before committing yourself to a particular course of action.

Bankers or shareholders outside the business will be more likely to be supportive if they see that the owner/manager knows what he wants to happen, and how to make it come about.

Most people who start up in business are fairly competitive. The budget acts as a standard against which they can measure their own business performance. This is particularly important for a new business in its first trading period, with no history to go on. In other words, you cannot really try to do better than last year, if there wasn't one. Thus, the only guide available is a realistic and achievable plan.

An attempt at planning invariably begs the question, 'How far ahead should I plan?' The answer, 'As far ahead as you can usefully see,' is not particularly helpful but it is the one most frequently given. Some guidelines that may help bring the planning horizon into view are:

(i)   Outsiders, such as bankers may have a standard period over which they expect you to plan, if you want to borrow money from them. Usually, this is at least three years, and for a new business preparing its first plan, three years is probably at the horizon itself.

(ii)   The Payback Period is another useful concept. If it is going to take you four or five years to recover your original investment and make a satisfactory profit, then that is how far you may want to plan. The payback period is a popular technique for evaluating capital investment decisions. It compares the cash cost of the initial investment with the annual net cash inflows (or savings) that are generated by the investment. This goes beyond simply calculating profit as shown in the Starlight Profit and Loss Account, which is governed by the realisation concept. The timing of the cash movements is calculated. That is, for example, when debtors will actually pay up, and when suppliers will have to be paid. By using cash in both elements, it is comparing like with like.

Table 3: Payback Period Method

DESIGNATION	$
Initial Cost of Project	10 000
Annual Net Cash Inflows	2 000
Year 1	2 000
Year 2	4 000
Year 3	4 000
Year 4	2 000
Year 5	1 000

The payback period is three years. That is when the $10 000 initial cash cost has been matched by the annual net cash inflows of $2 000; $4 000; $4 000 of the first three years.

(iii)   The Rate of Technology Change is yet another yardstick used in deciding how far ahead to plan. If your business is high-tech, or substantially influenced by changes in technology, then that factor must influence your choice of planning horizon. Companies in the early stages of the computer business which looked only three years ahead would have missed all the crucial technological trends, and as technological trends are vital factors influencing the success of any business in this field, the planning time horizon must accommodate them.

Every business must plan its first year in considerable detail. As well as a description of what the business is going to do, these plans should be summarised into month-by-month cash flows projection (in cash business such as a shop you may need to project cash flow on a weekly basis); a comprehensive quarterly Profit and Loss Account; and a full opening and closing position Balance Sheet. This first year plan is usually called the budget.

Jacob W. Chikuhwa

Future years could be planned in rather less detail, giving only quarterly cash flow projection, for example. If the planning horizon is very long, plans for the final years could be confined to statements about market (and technological) trends, anticipated market share and profit margins.

As a measure of business profitability, bankers usually look at profit margins. Any analysis of a business must consider the current level of sales activity. If you look at Starlight Profit and Loss Account (see Table 1), you will see that materials consumed in sales have jumped from $30 000 to $43 000 a rise of 43%. However, a quick look at the change in sales activity will show that the situation is nothing like so dramatic. Materials, as a percentage of sales, have risen from 30% to 33% (30 000/100 000 = 30% and 43 000/130 000 = 33%). Obviously, the more you sell, the more you must make.

To understand why there have been changes in the level of return on capital employed, we have to relate both profit and capital to sales activity. The ROCE equation can be expanded to look like this:

$$\frac{Profit}{Capital} = \frac{Profit}{Sales} \times \frac{Sales}{Capital}$$

This gives us two separate strands to examine — the profit strand and the capital strand. The first of these is usually called profit margins.

One final point before we look at how the budget and plans are prepared. There is a tendency to think of the budgeting process as a purely financial exercise, rather theoretical and remote from the day-to-day activity of the business. This is a serious misconception, usually fostered in larger companies, where the planners and the doers lead separate existences. People who have spent time in a large organisation have to recognise that in a small business, the decision maker has to prepare his own plans. No one likes to have someone else's plans foisted upon him, a useful point to remember if a small business has a number of decision takers working in it.

In the end, an entrepreneur needs the budget and plans expressed in financial terms: cash flow forecasts, profit and loss accounts and balance sheets. But the process of preparing the budget is firmly rooted in the real business world.

An Illustrative Budget System and Related Accounting Procedures

Financial planning and control processes perform a central role in implementing the general planning activities of a business. The financial planning and control manager analyses the sales growth of the business, the investment requirements to support planned growth, and the relations between revenues and costs, seeking to improve efficiency in the utilisation of funds for investment outlays and to maintain cost control as well. The budgeting processes represent a part of the broader financial planning and control systems. A complete budget system includes:

(i)   a production budget;
(ii)   a materials purchase budget;
(iii) a budgeted, or pro forma, income statement
(iv) a budgeted, or pro forma, balance sheet and
(v)   a capital expenditure budget.

The illustrative production budget (Table 4) is based directly on the sales forecast and the estimated unit cost of production. It is assumed that the firm maintains its finished goods inventory at 50% of the following month's sales. In any month, the firm must produce the unit sales plus ending inventory less the beginning inventory level.

Table 4: Production Budget (Estimated 2010, First Quarter)

ITEM	Monthly Average 2009	First Month	Second Month	Third Month	Source of Data
1. Sales at $10 per unit	$10 000	$10 000	$12 000	$12 000	Assumed
2. Unit Sales	1 000	1 000	1 200	1 200	Line 1 divided by $10
3. Beginning inventory (units)	500	500	600	600	1/2 of current month's sales
4. Difference (units)	500	500	600	600	Line 2 - Line3
5. Ending inventory (units)	500	500	600	600	1/2 of current month's sales
6. Production in units	1 000	1 100	1 200	1 200	Line 4 + Line 5
7. Estimated cost of goods					

produced	$6 000	$6 000	$7 200	$7 200	Line 6 x $6* per unit
8. Burden absorption, under		0	(100.)	(200.)	(200.)	Line 6 x $1 000 fixed manufacturing
or (over)					expense
9. Adjusted cost of goods	$6 000	$6 500	$7 000	$7 000	Line 7 less Line 8
9a. Adjusted cost per unit	**$6**	$5.91	$5.83	$5.83	Line 9 divided by Line 6
10. Value of ending inventory	$3 000	$3 545	$3 500	$3 500	Line 5 multiplied by Line
(finished goods)					9a (rounded)

*It has been assumed that cost of goods produced per unit = $6 and direct raw material cost $1 per unit.

The example illustrates the financial consequences of a rise in sales from $10 000-per-month level to a new plateau of $12 000. As production rises in response to increased sales, the (standard) cost of goods produced also rises. But the standard cost of goods produced increases faster than actual costs increase because of the unit cost of $6 per unit. An increase of one unit of production actually raises total costs by only $5. The estimated total cost, however, increases by $6. Estimates of the cost of goods produced are made and then adjusted by the amount of under- or over-absorbed burden. Of course, the same result for calculating the adjusted cost of goods produced (line 9 of Table 4) is obtained by multiplying $5 by the number of units produced to get total variable costs and adding $1 000 in fixed costs to reach total adjusted cost of goods produced.

The per unit adjusted costs of goods produced ($5.91) for the first month) is required to calculate the ending inventory. The first-in, first-out method of inventory costing is employed.

The level of operations indicated by the production budget is based on the sales forecast and inventory requirements. The materials purchase budget (Table 5) contains estimates of materials purchases that will be needed to carry out the production plans. Raw materials purchases depend in turn upon materials actually used in production, material costs, size of beginning inventories and requirements for ending inventory.

Table 5: Materials Purchase Budget

ITEM	Monthly Average 2009	First Month	Second Month	Third Month	Source of Data
11. Production in units	1 000	1 100	1 200	1 200	Line 6
12. Materials used (units)	2 000	2 200	2 400	2 400	Line 11 x 2
13. Raw materials, ending Inventory	2 200	2 400	2 400	2 400	Raw materials requirements next month
14. TOTAL	4 200	4 600	4 800	4 800	Line 12 + Line 13
15. Raw materials beginning Inventory	2 000	2 200	2 400	2 400	Raw materials requirements this month
16. Raw materials purchases	$2 200	$2 400	$2 400	$2 400	(Line 14 less Line 15) times $1

The example does not take into account economical ordering quantities (EOQs). EOQs are not integrated, primarily because they assume a uniform usage rate for raw materials, an assumption that is not met in the example. Also, the EOQs analysis assumes a constant minimum inventory, but the desired minimum inventory (line 13) shifts with production levels. In a practical situation, these assumptions might be approximated. EOQs could then be used to determine optimum purchase quantities, or more sophisticated operations research techniques might be used.

Companies that report a *pro forma* income statement or balance sheet usually do so because the events being excluded were unusual so the GAAP (Generally Accepted Accounting Principles) financial reports required by law or accounting standards are misleading to investors and potential investors. A hypothetical crisis that happened the previous quarter is not going to recur in future quarters, so the *pro forma* results can

Jacob W. Chikuhwa

be used by investors to forecast what a "regular" quarter might portend in the future.

The *pro forma* balance sheet, in particular, shows the projected book cash account; if all the other balance sheet accounts have transactions, *pro forma* figures and stock transactions of corporate managers. Managers must certify that they are responsible for establishing and maintaining internal controls and have designed such internal controls to ensure that material information relating to the company and its consolidated subsidiaries is made known to such managers by others within those entities, particularly during the period in which the periodic reports are being prepared.

Capital expenditure budgeting (or investment appraisal) is the planning process used to determine whether an organisation's long term investments such as new machinery, replacement machinery, new plants, new products, and research development projects are worth pursuing. It is a budget for major capital, or investment, expenditures.

For our purpose, we will look at the following budgets: the Cash Budget, the Budgeted Income Statement, and the Balance Sheet.

Considering Three Basic Budget Requirements

Cash Budget (Cash Flow Statement)

The purpose of budgeting is to provide a forecast of revenues and expenditures, i.e. construct a model of how your business might perform financially if certain strategies, events and plans are carried out. Secondly, it is to enable the actual financial operation of the business to be measured against the forecast. Thus, a cash flow/cash budget is a prediction of future cash receipts and expenditures for a particular time period. Its purpose is to manage the outflow of cash so that the business remains solvent. It usually covers a period in the short term future.

While traditionally the finance department compiles the company's budget, modern software allows hundreds or even thousands of people in various departments (operations, human resources, IT, etc.) to list their expected revenues and expenses in the final budget.

Using information developed in the production and materials purchase budgets, we can generate a cash budget. In addition, estimates for other expense categories are required. Only cash receipts from operations are considered, in order to emphasise the logic of the budget system. No account is taken of receipts or expenditures for capital items. This is because of the emphasis in this illustration on budgeting consequences of short-term fluctuations in the sales of the firm, although in practical situations it is a simple matter to incorporate capital expenditures into the Cash Budget. However, the fact that capital expenditures are ignored does not diminish their impact on cash flows. Capital expenditures occur sporadically and in amounts that sometimes overwhelm operating transactions.

Cash Budget Period

The three-month period used in the Cash Budget is not necessarily the length of the time for which a firm will predict cash flow. Although this period does coincide with the length of traditional ninety-day bank loans, a business is more likely to utilise a six-month or one-year period. Normally, a six-month forecast is prepared on a monthly basis. Briefly, the Cash Budget period will vary with the line of business, credit needs, the ability to forecast the firm's cash flows for the distant future, and requirements of funds.

Cash Budget Use

The cash flow budget helps the business determine when income will be sufficient to cover expenses and when the company will need to seek outside financing. The financial manager uses the Cash Budget to anticipate fluctuations in the level of cash. Normally, a growing business will be faced with continuous cash drains. The Cash Budget tells the manager the magnitude of the outflow. If necessary, he can plan to arrange for additional funds. The Cash Budget is the primary document presented to a lender to indicate the need for funds and the feasibility of repayments.

In our cash-budget example (Table 6), the opposite situation is illustrated. The business concern will have excess cash of at least $1 000 during each of the three months under consideration. The excess can be invested, or it can be used to reduce outstanding liabilities. In this example, the business retires notes payable (Budgeted Balance Sheet, Table 9, Line 49). Such a small amount as $1 000 may be held as cash or as a demand deposit, but the alert financial manager will not allow substantial amounts of cash to remain idle.

Jacob W. Chikuhwa

Table 6: Cash Budget (Estimated 2010, First Quarter)

ITEM	Monthly Average (2009)	First Month	Second Month	Third Month	Source of Data
RECEIPTS					
17. Accounts receivable					
Collected	$10 000	$10 000	$10 000	$12 000	Sales of previous month
DISBURSEMENTS					
18. Accounts payable paid	$2 000	$2 000	$2 400	$2 400	Raw materials purchases of previous month
19. Direct labour	$2 000	$2 200	$2 400	$2 400	Line 6 x $2
20. Indirect labour	$700	$700	$700	$700	Assumed
21. Variable manufacturing Expenses	1 000	1 100	1 200	1 200	Line 6 x $1
22. Insurance and taxes	100	100	100	100	Assumed
23. General and administrative Expenses	2 500	2 500	2 500	2 500	Assumed
24. Selling expenses	500	500	600	600	5% of Line 1
25. Total disbursements	$8 800	$9 300	$9 900	$9 900	Sum of Lines 18 through 24
26. Cash from operations	$1 200	$700	$100	$2 100	Line 17 less Line 25
26a. Initial cash	5 000	6 200	6 900	7 000	Preceding month, Line 26b
26b. Cumulative cash	6 200	6 900	7 000	9 100	Line 26 and Line 26a

27. Desired level of cash	5 000	5 000	6 000	6 000	5% of current month's Sales approx. 4.2% of annual sales
27a. Cash available (needed)					
cumulative	$1 200	$1 900	$1 000	$3 100	Line 26b less Line 27

After a cash budget has been developed, two additional financial statements can be formulated: the Budgeted Income Statement and the Budgeted Balance Sheet. They are prepared on an accrual rather than a cash basis. For example, the income statement accounts for depreciation charges. Expenses recognised on an accrual basis are included in total expenses (Table 7, Line 32); thus, calculated net income is lowered. The only accrual item assumed in this exhibit is depreciation, and this is assumed to be $200 monthly. The before-tax profit figure in the third month in the Budgeted Income Statement (Line 33) differs from Line 26 in the Cash Budget only by the amount of depreciation. This illustration makes clear the effect of non-cash expenses on the income statement.

Income Statement

The Budgeted Income Statement shows the impact of future events on the business's net income. Comparison of future income with that of past periods indicates the difficulties that will be encountered in maintaining or exceeding past performance. A forecast indicating low net income should cause management to increase sales efforts as well as to make efforts to reduce costs. Anticipation and prevention of difficulties can be achieved by a sound budgeting system.

Inventories have a significant effect on profits. A business that makes or buys goods to sell must keep track of inventories of goods under all accounting and income tax rules. Cost of goods sold (COGS) refer to the inventory costs of those goods a business has sold during a particular period (Table 8). Costs are associated with particular goods using one of several formulae, including specific identification, first-in first-out (FIFO), or average cost.

44

Jacob W. Chikuhwa

Table 7: Budgeted Income Statement

ITEM	Monthly Average 2009	First Month	Second Month	Third Month	Source of Data
28. Sales	$10 000	$10000	$12 000	$12 000	Line 17 less Line 25
29. Adjusted cost of sales	6 000	5 955	7 045	7 000	Line 40
30. Gross income	4 000	4 045	4 955	5 000	Line 28 less Line 29
31a. General and administrative Expenses	2 500	2 500	2 500	2 500	Line 23
31b. Selling expenses	500	500	600	600	5% of Line 1
32. Total expenses	$3 000	$3 000	$3 100	$3 100	Line 31a + Line 31b
33. Net income before taxes	1 000	1 040	1 855	1 900	Line 30 less Line 32
34. Government taxes	500	522	928	950	50% of Line 33
35. Net income after taxes	$500	$523	$927	$950	Line 33 less Line 34

Table 8: Worksheet (Adjusted Cost of Sales) [Estimated 2010, First Quarter]

ITEM	Monthly Average 2009	First Month	Second Month	Third Month	Source of Data
36. Adjusted cost of goods	$6 000	$6 500	$7 000	$7 000	Line 9
37. Add: Beginning inventory	3 000	3 000	3 545	3 500	Line 10 lagged one month
38. Sum	$9 000	$9 500	$10 545	$10 500	Line 36 + Line 37
39. Less: Ending inventory	3 000	3 545	3 500	3 500	Line 10

40. Adjusted cost of goods sold*	$6 000	$5955	$7045	$7 000	Line 38 less Line 39

* Note difference from Line 9, adjusted cost of goods produced.

Costs include all costs of purchase, costs of conversion and other costs incurred in bringing the inventories to their present location and condition. Costs of goods made by the business include material, labour, and allocated overhead. The costs of those goods not yet sold are deferred as costs of inventory until the inventory is sold or written down in value.

Balance Sheet

The Balance Sheet looks at the bigger picture of your business comparing all your assets to all your liabilities. It tells you if you closed the business and sold everything today, how much money would you have (or how much would you owe). The reason this is called a Balance Sheet is that Assets need to balance (equal) the Liabilities. The amount you would have if everything were liquidated today is called Net Worth and is listed under Liabilities. If you have more Liabilities than Assets, the Net Worth is negative.

Table 9: Budgeted Balance Sheet (Estimated 2010, First Quarter)

ITEM	Monthly Average 2009	First Month	Second Month	Third Month	Source of Data
ASSETS					
41. Cash	$5000	$5 000	$6 000	$6 000	Line 27
42. Government securities	-	-	-	-	-
43. Net receivables	10 000	10 000	12 000	12 000	Sales of current month
44. Inventories: Raw materials	2 200	2 400	2 400	2 400	Line 13
Finished goods	3 000	3 545	3 500	3 500	Line 10
45. Current assets	$20 200	$20 945	$23 900	$23 900	Total Lines 41

					through 44
46. Net fixed assets	80 000	79 800	79 600	79 400	$80 000 less $2 000
					depreciation per month
47. Total assets	$100 000	$100 745	$103 500	$103 300	Total Lines 45 and 46
LIABILITIES					
48. Accounts payable	$2 200	$2 400	$2 400	$2 400	Line 16
49. Notes payable, $3 200	2 000	1 300	2 200	100	$3 200 less Line 27a
50. Provision for Government					
income tax	500	1 022	1 950	2 900	Accumulation of Line 34
51. Long-term debt	25 000	25 000	25 000	25 000	Assumed
52. Common stock, $50 000	50 000	50 000	50 000	50 000	Assumed
53. Retained earnings, $20 000	20 000	21 023	21 950	22 900	Accumulation of Line 35 +
					$20 001
54. Total claims	$100 200	$100 745	$103 500	$103 300	Sum of Lines 48 through 53

The required information is readily available from past balance sheets or is contained in other elements of the budget system. For example, the initial balance of notes payable is $3 200. An increase in cash available (Line 27a) is used to repay notes payable, a decrease is met by additional borrowing from a commercial bank. Other new items, such as long-term debt and common stock (Lines 51 and 52), are taken from previous balance sheets.

A person who understands the logic and flow of this budget system can approach an actual budget with perspective looking for the fundamental relations involved and then applying the patterns to actual budget systems of any degree of complexity.

Budget Preparation and Budgetary Control

All large companies and government units, such as schools, use budgets as an aid in management planning and control. A budget is a written plan in action in numerical form, covering a specific period of time against which actual performance may be compared. The customary coverage for an operating budget is a year, which is then broken down into quarters or months. This breakdown is particularly important for firms that have seasonal variations although the major purpose is to allow for checking the budget against actual operations at frequent intervals.

Within a company, budgets typically are prepared for: sales, sales expenses and advertising, production in all major departments, cash and estimates of the financial statements. Preparation of any budget should be completed prior to the first day of the budget period. As operations move into the budgeted period, controls should be established so that corrective measures or revisions can be made promptly.

All the activities of a business depend primarily on the volume of sales. Thus, the first step in the preparation of a company budget is to establish the sales budget. All the other departmental budgets, such as the production budget are then set up on the basis of their relation to the sales budget.

Zero-Base Budgeting

In traditional budgeting, a manager simply adds to or subtracts from a previous year's budget to arrive at a new one. In recent years a new budgeting concept called zero-base budgeting (ZBB) has been adopted by some firms. ZBB requires the budget requests to be justified in detail from scratch — or zero each year. A manager must be able to show why any money should be spent at all.

A basic advantage of ZBB is the efficiency it brings to an organization. This is because ZBB requires the gathering of detailed information that helps managers to revaluate their operations.

In ZBB, projects are ranked and priorities are assigned. As a result, some projects are either eliminated, budgeted at a reduced level, budgeted at a similar level, or increased. ZBB attacks duplication and vested interests that have escaped serious review under the traditional budgeting methods.

Budgetary control is achieved by the use of tables or forms which show the budget figures for a period of time, such as a month, with a column for inserting actual performance reports as soon as they are compiled. A comparison (variation column) between the planned and actual results

Jacob W. Chikuhwa

indicates how well each department and the entire organisation are doing in measuring up to its budgeted figures. Any variations will be noted and corrective steps, if required, can be taken. For example, if sales in a certain territory are running below the budget, the sales manager can get in touch with the salespersons in that area to discover the cause of the trouble.

Auditing

In an on-going concern, the connection between audits, accounts and statistics is obvious. The main objective of an audit is to reveal loopholes in given control systems. Accounts involve the recording, classifying and summarising of business transactions, and the interpretation of this compiled information. One of the most commonly used methods for handling quantitative data is statistics. Business statistics deals with numerical (accounting) data related to the problems of business and, like accounts, involves: capturing (recording); checking; calculating and collation; presentation; and interpretation.

Thus, an audit is an independent opinion activity conducted within an organization for the review of its operations covered by its accounting system. An audit may be internal or external, depending on who is conducting it. In a Finance Department "housing" three branches, namely; accounts, internal audit and economics and statistics, an internal audit branch may act as a link between the accounts branch and the econo-stats branch. Specifically speaking, on revealing certain loopholes and/or irregularities in the accounting systems, the internal auditors should advise the econo-stats branch on the shortcomings and/or weaknesses in the accounting systems designed or forecasting methods applied for use in the financial forecasts and budget preparations by the accounts branch.

An external audit is an independent opinion activity executed by persons outside the organization. As well as being a periodic examination and evaluation of the accounting records of a business, it is conducted by a firm of certified public accountants.

When classified according to their subject matter, two common types of audits are the financial audit and the management audit. A special kind of audit — the corporate social audit — defines corporate social responsiveness.

Financial Audit

A financial audit is an examination and evaluation of the accounting systems and other monetary control systems of a firm. The auditors examine the accounting transactions in accordance with generally accepted auditing standards and designed media of recording of the accounts data. When deviations are found, the auditors suggest various corrective actions. Since so many measures of performance are based upon financial information, accurate financial records are necessary for effective managerial control.

Management Audit

A management audit is a detailed analysis of the overall operations of a company. It is concerned with the relationships among areas of the firm. Each activity of a company is carefully examined and evaluated. Actual performance is compared with expected performance. Inefficient operations can be identified so that improvements can be made. A management audit also serves as a check on the effectiveness of the other marginal controls.

Corporate Social Audit

A corporate social audit is a systematic attempt to measure and evaluate a corporation's impact on society. This audit may be conducted by internal or external auditors and may focus on a few or many of a company's activities. Further, the company's social performance may be reported in financial or non-financial terms. In the USA a social performance index was developed by the US Chamber of Commerce. This is a voluntary measure and guide to help firms see where they can be more socially active. This involves the types of social programmes a corporation decides to support. As areas of social involvements are established either by choice or by public pressure, companies will be expected to monitor and report carefully their social performance on a formal basis. Thus, some firms and trade groups already have their own social indexes; e.g. Arco has "The Social Critique", Pennsylvania Bank and Trust Company, "The Social Scorecard".

Jacob W. Chikuhwa

Basic Steps in Accounting Procedures

Accounts and business statistics involve seven basic steps. It should be noted that the most important function of business statics is to require the manager to explain situations or to state problems in a specific form.

(i) Data Capture: This is where figures and facts (data) are recorded on specially designed forms or source documents. Business transactions are entered in chronological order into a journal, which is a book of original entry. Although some small firms rely on pen-and-ink records, others use adding machines, cash registers, etc. Electronic data processing has made rapid strides in performing this first step as well as the other steps. Financial statements, purchase invoices, sales reports and payroll records can supply vital information that is subject to statistical analysis.

(ii) Data Checking: This involves the following operations: verifying of data which involves checking or validating of data to ensure that they were recorded correctly; classification of data which involves placing of data elements into specific categories which provide meaning for the user. For example, journal entries are transferred to a ledger. Here, each account brings together all transactions affecting one item such as cash or sales. At stated periods (monthly, quarterly, semi-annually, or annually) the ledger accounts are totalled, or balanced. These accounts provide the basic information for financial statements; arranging (sorting) of data which involves placing data elements in a specified or predetermined sequence; controlling of data which involves control to detect missing entries and illogical or unlikely entries.

(iii) Data Calculation: This is the step where data are input into the processing machine (an electronic calculator or a pocket calculator). Taken from the source documents or ledger, the figures are manipulated and processed. This involves: summarizing of data which involves combining or aggregating data elements into usable totals; processing of data which involves the arithmetic/logic manipulation of data to produce financial statements. Since these statements are the result of and the reason for much of the work done by an accounts branch, they are regarded essential management reports.

Various types of statistical measurements can be applied to produce results ready for presentation and interpretation. Two types of statistical measurement which are commonly used are ratios and percentages. Other common types of statistical measurement include averages, index numbers, correlations and time series.

(iv) Data Collation: After the essential management reports are processed, collation is carried out by way of reference to data already in files. This involves: controlling of data to check reasonableness and accuracy. Here data are compared with previous data of a similar nature; assembling of data in order to place the calculated data elements into a format that can be understood by the user. Such statements include the profit and loss statement, balance sheet, working capital statement, etc.

(v) Data Production: This is where the end product is produced (output). The manipulation and collation of the figures are complete and a statistical analysis is produced and stored or disseminated. The operations involved at this stage are analysis of data to reveal the full informational content of data, the underlying relationships they contain must be identified; storage of data which implies placing of data/information into some storage media such as paper, magnetic tape, magnetic disk or microfilm or USB, where it can be retrieved when needed; retrieval of data which involves the searching out and gaining access to specific data/information elements from the medium where it is stored; and reproduction of data which involves duplicating data/information from one medium to another or into another position in the same medium.

(vi) Data Interpretation: This is a vital step in business statistics that aids management to make decisions and to control operations. However, caution should be used in relying heavily on statistical measurements to influence decision making. Despite the best of intentions, several types of errors can creep into a computation. Arithmetic errors are likely to occur, particularly when the quality of data to be processed is extensive.

(vii) Data Presentation: This involves showing of results in a form that is easily understood. To present statistical material in a manner that will be useful for purposes of analysis, two devices are commonly used. These are summary tables and graphic presentations. The graphic presentation of statistical data has the great advantage of presenting a visual analysis of the facts. Examples of graphic statistical presentations are the line or curve chart, the bar chart, the pie diagram or circular chart.

Jacob W. Chikuhwa

The objectives in this final step in accounting procedures should be three fold, namely:
(a) to convey an entirely unexpected input to management;
(b) to reduce uncertainty about a future state of event. The interpretation should bring new understanding about a future state of event. The interpretation should bring new understanding by modifying the original perception; and/or
(c) to increase the knowledge level of the recipient. The fact that a business may or may not have been operated at a profit is of vital concern, but this one figure fails to tell the whole story. For example, a bank may be willing to extend a loan to a firm that has a strong financial structure despite recent operating losses. Judicious use of such borrowed funds might correct conditions so that future business operations would be profitable. On the other hand, a firm may be headed for financial trouble even though it is currently operating profitably. Therefore, one has to take a candid approach when interpreting accounting/statistical data.

Costing for Business Start-up

Paradoxically, one of the main reasons small businesses fail in the early stages is that too much start-up capital is used to buy fixed assets. While clearly some equipment is essential at the start, other purchases could be postponed. This may mean that 'desirable' and labour saving devices have to be borrowed or hired for a specific period. Obviously, not as nice as having them to hand all the time but if, for example, photocopiers, electronic typewriters, word processors, micros and even delivery vans are bought into business, they become part of the fixed costs. The higher the fixed cost plateau, the longer it usually takes to reach break-even and then profitability. And time is not usually on the side of the small new business. It has to become profitable relatively quickly or it will simply run out of money and die.

Costs for a start-up business can be divided up into six major categories:
(i)   Cost of Sales: Product inventory, raw materials, manufacturing equipment, shipping, packaging, shipping insurance, warehousing;
(ii)   Professional Fees: Setting up a legal structure for your business (e.g. Limited Liability Company, corporation), trademarks,

copyrights, patents, drafting partnership and non-disclosure agreements, attorney fees for on-going consultation, retaining an accountant;

(iii) Technology Costs: Capital equipment (e.g. machinery/plant, computer hardware, computer software, printers, security measures, IT consulting);

(iv) Administrative Costs: Various types of business insurance, office supplies, licenses and permits, express shipping and postage, product packaging, parking, rent, utilities, phones, copier, fax machine, desks, chairs, filing cabinets – anything else you need to have on a daily basis to operate a business;

(v) Sales and Marketing Costs: Printing of stationery, marketing materials, advertising, public relations, event or trade show attendance or sponsorship, trade association or chamber of commerce membership fees, travel and entertainment for client meetings, mailing or lead lists;

(vi) Wages and Benefits: Employee salaries, payroll taxes, benefits, workers compensation.

We are going to look at two hypothetical new small businesses (Table 10). They are both making and selling identical products at the same price, $10. They plan to sell 10 000 units each in the first year. The owner of Company A plans to get fully equipped at the start. His fixed costs will be $40 000, double that of Company B. This is largely because, as well as his own car, he has bought such things as a delivery van, new equipment and a photocopier. Much of this will not be fully used for some time, but will save some money now. This extra expenditure will result in a lower unit variable cost than Company B can achieve a typical capital intensive result. Company B's owner, on the other hand, proposes to start up on a shoestring. Only $20 000 will go into fixed costs, but of course, his unit variable cost will be higher, at $4.50. The variable cost is higher because, for example, he has to pay an outside carrier to deliver, while Company A uses his own van and pays only for petrol.

Jacob W. Chikuhwa

Table 10: Costing for Business Start-up

Company A

ITEM	DATA ($)
Unit variable cost	2,5
Fixed costs	40 000
Variable costs	25 000
Total costs	65 000
Selling price	10,0
Break-even point	40 000/(10-2,5) = 5333 units
Profit at Maximum Volume (Sales Revenue - Total Costs)	35 000

Company B

ITEM	DATA ($)
Unit variable cost	4,5
Fixed costs	20 000
Variable costs	45 000
Total costs	65 000
Selling price	10,0
Break-even point	20 000/(10-4,5) = 3636 units
Profit at Maximum Volume	35 000

From the data on each company you can see that total costs for 10 000 units are the same, so total possible profits, if 10 000 units are sold are also the same. The key difference is that Company B starts making profits after 3 636 units have been sold. Company A has to wait until 5 333 units have been sold.

Financial Control

Another pair of reasons why small businesses fail very early on is connected with the market place. They are frequently over-optimistic on how much they can sell. They also under-estimate how long it takes for sales to build up. So for these reasons, and spending too much start-up capital on fixed assets, great care should be taken to keep start-up fixed costs to the minimum.

There are all sorts of 'persuasive' arguments to go for a capital intensive cost structure. In periods of high growth, the greater margin on sales will produce a higher ROCE, but high fixed costs will always expose a new or small business to higher risks. A small business has enough risks to face, with a survival rate of less than 20 percent in its first few years, without adding them.

Book-keeping

The entrepreneur has now made up his/her mind to go into business. However, it is significant to know the principles and systems of book-keeping necessary to survive in business. Choosing the form of his/her business is now a foregone conclusion.

One must understand that book-keeping is the recording of financial transactions. These transactions include sales, purchases, income, and payments by an individual or organisation. Book-keeping is usually performed by a book-keeper, but it should not be confused with accounting. The accounting process is usually performed by an accountant. The accountant creates reports from the recorded financial transactions recorded by the book-keeper and files forms with government agencies.

Thus, a book-keeper, also known as an accounting clerk or accounting technician, is a person who records the day-to-day financial transactions of an organisation. A book-keeper is usually responsible for writing the "daybooks". These daybooks consist of purchases, sales, receipts, and payments. The bookkeeper is responsible for ensuring all transactions are recorded in the correct daybook, suppliers' ledger, customer ledger and general ledger. The bookkeeper brings the books to the trial balance stage. An accountant may prepare the income statement and balance sheet using the trial balance and ledgers prepared by the bookkeeper

Jacob W. Chikuhwa

It is hard to believe that any businessman could hope to survive without knowing how much cash he has and what his profit or loss on sales is. He needs these facts on at least a monthly, weekly, or occasionally even a daily basis, to survive yet alone to grow.

In simple terms, the main reasons for book-keeping are:

(i)   to keep records of income (money coming in) and expenditure (money spent) so that the profit or loss during a period of time can be easily worked out;

(ii)   to keep records of assets (property and stock owned) and liabilities (bills or money still owing to others) so that the financial situation of the project or business can be worked out at any time.

The owner/manager may keep the books himself at the start, if the business is small and the trading methods simple. Later on, he may feel his time could be more usefully spent helping the business to expand. At that stage, he may have a book-keeper in for a few hours, or days, a week. Or perhaps he could use an outside book-keeping service, sending the information to them periodically.

Many small retailers now have cash tills that are programmed to analyse sales, produce product gross margin information, stock levels, and even signed when and how much new stock is needed. Finally, if the work and profits warrant it, a book-keeper (or even an accountant) may be employed full time.

The Records to be Kept

The records must keep track of all items that affect both cash and profits.

The emergence of computerised systems has created the possibility of on-line book-keeping. Online book-keeping, or remote bookkeeping, allows source documents and data to reside in web-based applications which allow remote access for book-keepers and accountants. All entries made into the on-line software are recorded and stored in a remote location. The on-line software can be accessed from any location in the world and permit the book-keeper or data entry person to work from any location with a suitable data communications link.

There are two main methods for keeping the accounts of small businesses. These are single-entry book-keeping and double-entry book-keeping. Their names really explain themselves. The primary book-keeping record in *single-entry bookkeeping* is the cash book, which is similar to a checking (cheque) account register but allocates the income and expenses to various income and expense accounts. Separate account records are maintained for petty cash, accounts payable and receivable, and other relevant transactions such as inventory and travel expenses. These days, single-entry book-keeping can be done with DIY bookkeeping software to speed up manual calculations.

In *double-entry book-keeping*, for every entry recorded, it is in fact recorded twice, whereas in single entry book-keeping, it is just recorded once. The double-entry book-keeping method is advantageous in that when mistakes and/or distortions happen (and they always do) they are much easier to find. This method can also deal with unpaid bills and accounts.

Table 11: Double-entry Book-keeping

Transaction	*Debit*	*Credit*
Cash	1 640	
Accounts receivable	450	
Sales		1 700
Accounts receivable		315
Sales tax payable		75

When one becomes more comfortable with bookkeeping entries, one could simplify the above entry slightly by "netting" the change in accounts receivable for the day, as shown in the table below.

Table 12: Simplified Double-entry Book-keeping

Transaction	*Debit*	*Credit*
Cash	1 640	
Accounts receivable	135	
Sales		1 700
Sales tax payable		75

Jacob W. Chikuhwa

This is a method of keeping accounting records that recognises the dual nature (source and disposition) of every financial transaction expressed by the basic accounting equation (Assets = Liabilities + Owners' Equity). In this method, every transaction is entered twice in the account books first, to record a change in the assets' side (called a 'debit') and, second, to mirror that change in the equities' side (called a 'credit').

If all entries are recorded accurately, the account books will 'balance' because the total of debit entries will equal the total of credit entries. Double-entry book-keeping is used universally, except in very small or cash-transactions based firms which use 'single-entry book-keeping'.

In order to take control of financial recordkeeping, a businessperson must accurately record day-to-day sales, purchases, and other transactions. A daybook is a descriptive and chronological (diary-like) record of day-to-day financial transactions also called a *book of original entry*. The daybook's details must be entered formally into journals to enable posting to ledgers. Daybooks include:

(i)   Sales and revenue daybook, for recording all the sales and revenue invoices;

(ii)   Sales credits daybook, for recording all the sales credit notes;

(iii)   Purchases daybook, for recording all the purchase invoices;

(iv)   Purchases credits daybook, for recording all the purchase credit notes;

(v)   Cash daybook, usually known as the cash book, for recording all money received as well as money paid out. It may be split into two daybooks: receipts daybook for money received in, and payments daybook for money paid out.

And then there is a journal which is a formal and chronological record of financial transactions before their values are accounted for in the general ledger as debits and credits. A company can maintain one journal for all transactions, or keep several journals based on similar activity (i.e. sales, cash receipts, revenue, etc.) making transactions easier to summarize and reference later. For every debit journal entry recorded, there must be an equivalent credit journal entry to maintain a balanced accounting equation.

There are many software solutions on the market to help with the automation of accounting procedures. Accounting software is sold in office supply stores, software outlets, electronics stores, mail order houses, and directly from software publishers. It is advisable to look for accounting software that permits the use of passwords to control access to all or some of the business's accounting transactions.

Closing the Books

When you reach the end of an accounting period, you need to "close the books." At a minimum, you will close your books annually because you have to file an income tax return every year. If you are having financial statements prepared, you will want them done at least annually. However, annual financial statements may not be enough to help you keep tabs on your business. You may want financial statements monthly, bi-monthly, or quarterly.

Even if you are not having financial statements prepared, you may want to close your books monthly. Sending out customer statements, paying your suppliers, reconciling your bank statement, and submitting sales tax reports to the State are probably some of the tasks you need to do every month. You may find it easier to do these if you close your books.

How to close your books: After you finish entering the day-to-day transactions in your journals, you are ready to "close the books" for the period. A step-by-step description of how to close the books follows. How many of the steps you do yourself depends on how much of the accounting you want to do, and how much you want to pay your accountant to do.

(i)   Post entries to the general ledger: Transfer the account totals from your journals (sales and cash receipts journal and cash disbursements journal) to your general ledger accounts.

(ii)   Total the general ledger accounts: By footing the general ledger accounts, you will arrive at a preliminary ending balance for each account.

(iii)   Prepare a preliminary trial balance: Add all of the general ledger account ending balances together. Total debits should equal total credits. This will help assure you that your accounts balance prior to making adjusting entries.

(iv)   Prepare adjusting journal entries: Certain end-of-period adjustments must be made before you can close your books. Adjusting entries are required to account for items that do not get recorded in your daily transactions. In a traditional accounting system, adjusting entries are made in a general journal.

Jacob W. Chikuhwa

(v)   Foot the general ledger accounts again: This will give you the adjusted balance of each general ledger account.
(vi)   Prepare an adjusted trial balance: Prepare another trial balance, using the adjusted balances of each general ledger account. Again, total debits must equal total credits.
(vii)   Prepare financial statements: After tracking down and correcting any trial balance errors, you (or your accountant) are ready to prepare a balance sheet and income statement.
(viii) Prepare closing entries: Get your general ledger ready for the next accounting period by clearing out the revenue and expense accounts and transferring the net income or loss to owner's equity. This is done by preparing journal entries that are called closing entries in a general journal.
(ix)   Prepare a post-closing trial balance: After you make closing entries, all revenue and expense accounts will have a zero balance. Prepare one more trial balance. Since all revenue and expense accounts have been closed out to zero, this trial balance will only contain balance sheet accounts. Remember that the total debit balance must equal the total credit balance. This will help ensure that all general ledger account balances are correct as of the beginning of the new accounting period.

(For information on the Trial Balance, read A Handbook in Business Management.)

Choosing the Form of Your Business

At the outset of your business venture, you will have to decide in what legal form to establish your business. That form will significantly influence the types of money that are available to you. There are four main forms that a business can take, with a number of variations on two of these. The form that you choose will depend on a number of factors: Commercial needs, financial risk and your tax position. All play an important part.

(i) Sole Trader

If you have the facilities, cash and customers, you can start trading under your own name immediately. There are no rules about the records you have to keep neither is there requirement for an external audit, or for financial information on your business to be filed with the Registrar of Companies. You would be prudent to keep good books and to get professional advice, as you will have to declare your income to the Income Tax Department.

Without good records you will lose in any dispute over tax. You are personally liable for the debts of your business, and in the extent of your business failing, your personal possessions can be sold to meet them.

A sole trader does not have access to equity capital, which has the attraction of being risk-free to the business. He must rely on loans from banks or individuals and any other non-equity source of finance.

(ii) Partnership

There are very few restrictions to setting up in business with another person or persons in partnership. Many partnerships are formed without legal formalities, and sometimes drifted into without the parties themselves being aware that they have entered a partnership. All that is needed is for two or more people to agree to carry on a business together intending to share the profits. The law will then recognise the existence of a partnership.

Most of the points raised when considering sole tradership apply equally to partnerships. All the partners are personally liable for the debts of the business, even if those debts were incurred by one partner's mismanagement or dishonesty without the other partner's knowledge. Even death may not release a partner from his obligations, and in some circumstances his estate can remain liable. Unless you take 'public' leave of your partnership by notifying your business contacts, and advertising retirement in the Financial Gazette, you will remain liable indefinitely. So it is vital before entering a partnership to be absolutely sure of your partner and to take legal advice in drawing up a contract, which should cover the following points:

Profit Sharing, Responsibilities and Duration — this should specify how profits and losses are to be shared, and who is to carry out which tasks. It should also set limits on partner's monthly drawings, and on how long the partnership itself is to last (either a specific period of years or indefinitely, with a cancellation period of, say three months).

Voting Rights and Policy Decision — unless otherwise stated, all the partners have equal voting rights. It is advisable to get a definition of what

Jacob W. Chikuhwa

is a policy or voting decision, and how such decisions are to be made. You must also decide how to expel or admit a new partner.

Time Off — every partner is entitled to his share of the profits, even when ill or on holiday. You will need some guidelines on the length and frequency of holidays, and on what to do if someone is absent for a long period for any other reasons.

Withdrawing Capital — you have to decide how each partner's share of the capital of the business will be valued in the event of a partner leaving or the partnership being dissolved.

Accountancy Procedures — you do not have either to file accounts or to have accounts audited. However, it may be prudent to agree a satisfactory standard of accounting and have a firm of accountants to carry out that work. Sleeping partners may well insist on it.

Sleeping Partners — a partner who has put up capital but does not intend to take an active part in running the business can protect himself against risks by having his partnership registered as a limited partnership.

(iii) Limited Company

The main distinction between a limited company and either sole tradership or partnership is that it has a legal identity of its own separate from the people who own it. This means that, in the event of liquidation, creditors' claims are restricted to the assets of the company. The shareholders are not liable as individuals for the business debts beyond the paid-up value of their shares. This applies even if the shareholders are working directors, unless the company has been trading fraudulently.

Other advantages include the freedom to raise capital by selling shares and certain tax concessions.

The disadvantages include the legal requirement for the company's accounts to be audited by a chartered or certified accountant and for certain records of the business trading activities to be filed annually with the Registrar of Companies.

A limited company can be formed by two shareholders, one of whom must be a director. A company secretary must also be appointed, who can be a shareholder, director, or an outside person such as an accountant.

The company can be bought 'off the shelf' from a registration agent then adapted to suit your own purposes. This will involve changing the name, shareholders and article of association. Alternatively, you can form you own company, using your solicitor or accountant.

iv) Cooperative

There is an alternative form of business for people whose primary concern is to create a democratic work environment, sharing profits and control. If you want to control or substantially influence your own destiny, and make as large a capital gain out of your life's work as possible, then a cooperative is not for you.

The membership of the cooperative is the legal body that controls the business, and members must work in the business. Each member has one vote, and the cooperative must be registered under the Cooperatives Act.

Preparing Your Business Plan

Now that you have chosen your form of business, it's time to prepare your business plan to be presented to prospective bankers and investors. Bankers or investors will show an interest if they see that the owner/manager knows what he or she has in mind.

1. Executive Summary

The executive summary is often considered the most important section of a business plan. This section briefly tells interested bankers and prospective shareholders where your company is, where you want to take it, and why your business idea will be successful. If you are seeking financing, the executive summary is also your first opportunity to grab a potential investor's interest.

The executive summary should highlight the strengths of your overall plan and therefore be the last section you write. However, it usually appears first in your business plan document.

What to Include in the Executive Summary

Based on the stage of development of your business, several key points that should form part of the executive summary (whether yours is an established or start-up new business) include:

Jacob W. Chikuhwa

An Established Business

➢ The Mission Statement — this explains what your business is all about. It should be between several sentences and a paragraph.

➢ Company Information — include a short statement that covers when your business was formed, the names of the founders and their roles, number of employees, and your business location.

➢ Growth Highlights — include examples of company growth, such as financial or market highlights (for example, increased profit margins and market share year-over-year since its foundation). Graphs and charts can be helpful in this section.

➢ Your Products/Services — briefly describe the products or services you provide.

➢ Financial Information — if you are seeking financing, include any information about your current bank and investors.

➢ Summarize future plans — explain where you would like to take your business.

With the exception of the mission statement, all of the information in the executive summary should be covered in a concise fashion and kept to one page. Because the executive summary is the first part of your business plan many interested people will see, each word should count.

A Start-up or New Business

If you are just starting a business, you won't have as much information as an established company. Instead, focus on your experience and background as well as the decisions that led you to start this particular enterprise.

Demonstrate that you have done a thorough market analysis. Include information about a demand or gap in your target market, and how your particular solutions can fill it. Convince the interested reader that you can succeed in your target market, then address your future plans.

NB! Remember, your Executive Summary will be the last thing you write.

2. Company Description

This section of your business plan provides a high-level review of the different elements of your business. This is akin to an extended elevator pitch and can help interested readers and potential investors quickly understand the goals and objectives of your business and its unique proposition.

What to Include in the Company Description

➤ Describe the nature of your business and list the marketplace needs that you are trying to satisfy.
➤ Explain how your products and services meet these needs.
➤ List the specific consumers, organizations or businesses that your company serves or will serve.
➤ Explain the competitive advantages that you believe will make your business a success such as your location, expert personnel, efficient operations, or ability to bring value to your customers.

3. Market Analysis

The next step in writing a business plan is a market analysis. The market analysis section of your business plan should illustrate your industry and market knowledge as well as any of your research findings and conclusions.

What to include in the Market Analysis

➤ Industry description and outlook — Describe your industry, including its current size and historic growth rate as well as other trends and characteristics (e.g., life cycle stage, projected growth rate). Next, list the major customer groups within your industry.
➤ Information about your target market — Narrow your target market to a manageable size. Many businesses make the mistake of trying to appeal to too many target markets. Research and include the following information about your market:

Jacob W. Chikuhwa

(a)   Distinguishing characteristics — what are the critical needs of your potential customers? Are those needs being met? What are the demographics of the group and where are they located? Are there any seasonal or cyclical purchasing trends that may impact your business?

(b)   Size of the primary target market — in addition to the size of your market, what data can you include about the annual purchases your market makes in your industry? What is the forecasted market growth for this group?

(c)   How much market share can you gain? — what is the market share percentage and number of customers you expect to obtain in a defined geographic area? Explain the logic behind your calculation.

(d)   Pricing and gross margin targets — define your pricing structure, gross margin levels, and any discount that you plan to use.

When you include information about any of the market tests or research studies you have completed, be sure to focus only on the results of these tests. Any other details should be included in the appendix.

➢ Competitive Analysis — your competitive analysis should identify your competition by product line or service and market segment. Assess the following characteristics of the competitive landscape:
(a) Market share
(b) Strengths and weaknesses
(c) How important is your target market to your competitors?
(d) Are there any barriers that may hinder you as you enter the market?
(e) What is your window of opportunity to enter the market?
(f) Are there any indirect or secondary competitors who may impact your success?
(g) What barriers to market are there (e.g., changing technology, high investment cost, lack of qualified personnel)?

➤ Regulatory restrictions — include any customer or governmental regulatory requirements affecting your business, and how you will comply. Also, cite any operational or cost impact the compliance process will have on your business.

4. Organisation and Management

Organization and Management follows the Market Analysis. This section should include: your company's organisation structure, details about the ownership of your company, profiles of your management team, and the qualifications of your Board of Directors (if you have a Board of Directors).

Who does what in your business? What is their background and why are you bringing them into the business as board members or employees? What are they responsible for? These may seem like unnecessary questions to answer in a one- or two-person organization, but the interested people reading your business plan want to know who is in charge. Give a detailed description of each division or department and its function.

This section should include what kind of salary and benefits package you have for your employees. What incentives are you offering? What promotion prospects are there? Reassure your interested reader that the people you have on staff are more than just names on a letterhead.

➤ Organisation Structure

A simple but effective way to lay out the structure of your company is to create an organisation chart with a narrative description. This will prove that you are leaving nothing to chance, you have thought out exactly who is doing what, and there is someone in charge of every function of your company. Nothing will fall through the cracks, and nothing will be duplicated. To a potential investor or employee, that is very important.

➤ Ownership Information

Jacob W. Chikuhwa

This section should also include the legal structure of your business along with the subsequent ownership information it relates to. Have you incorporated your business? If so, is it a corporation or limited liability? Or perhaps you have formed a partnership with someone. If so, is it a general or limited partnership? Or maybe you are a sole trader.

The following important ownership information should be incorporated into your business plan:

(a) Names of owners
(b) Percentage ownership
(c) Extent of involvement with the company
(d) Forms of ownership (i.e., common stock, preferred stock, general partner, limited partner)
(e) Outstanding equity equivalents (i.e., options, warrants, convertible debt)
(f) Common stock (i.e., authorized or issued)
(g) Management Profiles

➤ Management Information

Experts agree that one of the strongest factors for success in developing a company is the ability and track record of its owner/management team. Therefore, make sure an interested reader gets to know the profiles of the key people in the company. Provide resumes (CVs) that include the following information:

(a) (a) Name
(b) Position (include brief position description along with primary duties)
(c) Primary responsibilities and authority
(d) Education
(e) Unique experience and skills
(f) Previous employment
(g) Special skills
(h) Past track record
(i) Industry recognition
(j) Community involvement
(k) Number of years with company

(l) Compensation basis and levels (make sure these are reasonable — not too high or too low)
(m) Be sure you quantify achievements (e.g. "Managed a sales force of ten people," "Managed a department of fifteen people," "Increased revenue by 15% in the first six months," "Expanded the retail outlets at the rate of two each year," "Improved the customer service as rated by our customers from a 60% to a 90% rating.")

Also highlight how the people surrounding you complement your own skills. If you are just starting out, show how each person's unique experience will contribute to the success of your venture.

➤ Board of Directors' Qualifications

The major benefit of an unpaid advisory board is that it can provide expertise that your company cannot otherwise afford. A list of well-known, successful business owners/managers can go a long way towards enhancing your company's credibility and perception of management expertise.

If you have a Board of Directors, be sure to gather the following information when developing the outline for your business plan:

(a) Names
(b) Positions on the board
(c) Extent of involvement with company
(d) Background
(e) Historical and future contribution to the company's success

5. Service or Product Line

Once you have completed the Organisation and Management section of your plan, the next part of your business plan is where you describe your service or product, emphasising the benefits to potential and current customers. Focus on why your particular product will satisfy a need for your target customers.

Jacob W. Chikuhwa

What to include in the Service or Product Section

➤ A Description of your product/service — include information about the specific benefits of your product or service — from your customers' perspective. You should also talk about your product or service's ability to meet consumer needs, any advantages your product has over that of competitors, and the current development stage your product is in (e.g., idea, prototype).

➤ Details about your Product's life cycle — be sure to include information about where your product or service is in its life cycle, as well as any factors that may influence its cycle in future.

➤ Intellectual property — if you have any existing, pending, or any anticipated copyright or patent filings, list them here. Also disclose whether any key aspects of a product may be classified as trade secrets. Last, include any information pertaining to existing legal agreements, such as nondisclosure or non-compete agreements.

➤ Research and Development (R&D) activities — outline any R&D activities that you are involved in or are planning. What results of future R&D activities do you expect? Be sure to analyse the R&D efforts of not only your own business, but also of others in your industry.

6. Marketing and Sales

Once you have completed the Service or Product Line section of your plan, the next part of your business plan should focus on your marketing and sales management strategy for your business.

Marketing is the process of creating customers, and customers are the lifeblood of your business. In this section, the first thing you want to do is define your marketing strategy. There is no single way to approach a marketing strategy; your strategy should be part of an on-going business-evaluation process and unique to your company. However, there are common steps you can follow which will help you think through the direction and tactics you would like to use to drive sales and sustain customer loyalty.

An overall marketing strategy should include four different strategies:

➢ A market penetration strategy.

➢ A growth strategy — this strategy for building your business might include:

    (a) an internal strategy such as how to increase your human resources,

    (b) an acquisition strategy such as buying another business,

    (c) a franchise strategy for branching out,

    (d) a horizontal strategy where you would provide the same type of products to different users,

    (e) or a vertical strategy where you would continue providing the same products but would offer them at different levels of the distribution chain.

➢ Channels of distribution strategy — choices for distribution channels could include:

    (a) original equipment manufacturers (OEMs),

    (b) an internal sales force,

    (c) distributors, or retailers.

➢ Communication strategy — how are you going to reach your customers? Usually a combination of the following tactics works the best:

    (a) promotions,

    (b) advertising,

    (c) public relations,

    (d) personal selling,

    (e) printed materials such as brochures, catalogues, flyers, etc.

After you have developed a comprehensive marketing strategy, you can then define your sales strategy. This covers how you plan to actually sell your product.

Your overall sales strategy should include two primary elements:

➢ A sales force strategy — if you are going to have a sales force, do you plan to use internal or independent representatives? How many salespeople will you recruit for your sales force? What type of recruitment strategies will you use? How will you train your sales force? What about compensation for your sales force?

Jacob W. Chikuhwa

➤ Your sales activities — when you are defining your sales strategy, it is important that you break it down into activities. For instance, you need to identify your prospects. Once you have made a list of your prospects, you need to prioritise the contacts, selecting the leads with the highest potential to buy first. Next, identify the number of sales calls you will make over a certain period of time. From there, you need to determine the average number of sales calls you will need to make per sale, the average dollar size per sale, and the average dollar size per vendor.

7. Funding Request

If you are seeking funding for your business venture, use this section to outline your requirements.

Your funding request should include the following information:

➤ Your current funding requirements
➤ Any future funding requirements over the next five years
➤ How you intend to use the funds you receive: Is the funding request for capital expenditures? Working capital? Debt retirement? Acquisitions? Whatever it is, be sure to list it in this section.
➤ Any strategic financial situational plans for the future, such as: a buyout, being acquired, debt repayment plan, or selling your business. These areas are extremely important to a future creditor, since they will directly impact your ability to repay your loan(s).

When you are outlining your funding requirements, include the amount you want now and the amount you want in future. Also include the time period that each request will cover, the type of funding you would like to have (e.g., equity, debt), and the terms that you would like to have applied.

To support your funding request, you will also need to provide historical and prospective financial information.

8. Financial Projections

You should develop the Financial Projections section after you have analysed the market and set clear objectives. That is when you can allocate resources efficiently. The following is a list of the critical financial statements to include in your business plan package.

➤ Historical Financial Data — if you own an established business, you will be requested to supply historical data related to your company's performance. Most creditors request data for the last three to five years, depending on the length of time you have been in business. The historical financial data to be included are your company's cash flow statements, income statements and balance sheets for each year you have been in business (usually for up to three to five years). Often, creditors are also interested in any collateral that you may have that could be used as security for your loan, regardless of the stage of your business.

➤ Prospective Financial Data — all businesses, whether start-up or established, will be required to supply prospective financial data. Most of the time, creditors will want to see what you expect your company to be able to do within the next five years. Each year's documents should include forecasted cash flow statements, income statements, balance sheets and capital expenditure budgets. For the first year, you should supply monthly or quarterly projections. After that, you can stretch it to quarterly and/or yearly projections for years two through five. Make sure your projections match your funding requests; creditors will be on the lookout for inconsistencies. It is much better if you detect mistakes before they do. If you have made assumptions in your projections, be sure to summarize what you have assumed. This way, the interested reader will not be left guessing.

➤ Finally, include a short analysis of your financial information. Include a ratio and trend analysis for all of your financial statements (both historical and prospective). Since pictures speak louder than words, you may want to add graphs of your trend analysis (especially if they are positive).

Jacob Chikuhwa

9. Appendix

The Appendix should be provided to interested parties on a request basis. In other words, it should not be included with the main body of your business plan. Your plan is your communication tool; as such, it will be seen by a lot of people. Some of the information in the Appendix section will be confidential, but specific individuals (such as creditors) may want access to this information to make lending decisions. Therefore, it is important to have the Appendix within easy reach.

The Appendix would include:
- Credit history (personal & business)
- Resumes of key managers
- Product pictures
- Letters of reference
- Details of market studies
- Relevant magazine articles or book references
- Licenses, permits or patents
- Legal documents
- Copies of leases
- Building permits
- Contracts
- List of business consultants, including attorney and accountant

Any copies of your business plan should be controlled; keep a distribution record. This will allow you to update and maintain your business plan on a request basis. Remember, too, that you should include a private placement disclaimer with your business plan if you plan to use it to raise capital.

10. How to Make Your Business Plan Visible

One of the first steps to business planning is determining your target market and why they would want to buy from you. For example, is the market you serve the best one for your product or service? Are the benefits of dealing with your business clear and are they aligned with customer needs? If you are unsure about the answers to any of these questions, take a step back and revisit the foundation of your business plan.

The following tips can help you clarify what your business has to offer, identify the right target market for it and build a niche for yourself.

➤ Be clear about what you have to offer — ask yourself what you are really selling beyond basic products or services. Consider this example: Your town probably has several restaurants all selling one fundamental product — food. But each is targeted at a different need or clientele. One might be a drive-in fast food restaurant, perhaps another sells pizza in a rustic Italian kitchen, and maybe there is a fine dining seafood restaurant that specialises in wood-grilled fare. All these restaurants sell meals, but they sell them to targeted clientele looking for the unique qualities each has to offer. What they are *really* selling is a combination of product, value, ambience and brand experience.

When starting a business, be sure to understand what makes your business unique. What needs does your product or service fulfil? What benefits and differentiators will help your business stand out from the crowd?

➤ Don't be a Jack-of-all-trades (learn to strategize) — it is important to clearly define what you are selling or service you are providing. You do not want to become a jack-of-all-trades and master of none because this can have a negative impact on business growth. As a small business, it is often a better strategy to divide your products or services into manageable market niches. Small operations can then offer specialised goods and services that are attractive to a specific group of prospective buyers.

➤ Identify your niche — creating a niche for your business is essential to success. Often, business owners can identify a niche based on their own market knowledge, but it can also be helpful to conduct a market survey with potential customers to uncover untapped needs. During your research process, identify the following:
(a) Which areas are your competitors already well-established?
(b) Which areas are being ignored by your competitors?

Jacob W. Chikuhwa

(c) What potential opportunities are there for your business that can be exploited?

DATA PROCESSING CONCEPTS

Data processing is a specialist activity concerned with the systematic recording, arranging, processing, filing and dissemination of facts relating to the physical events (transactions and other) occurring in the business.

Whereas the factory processes raw materials and produce goods for sale, a data processing department (section) processes basic data and produces basic business documents and control information for management to keep them informed of events within the business; this enables them to coordinate different activities of the organisation's functional groups and to control the day-to-day transactions and be in a position to take whatever corrective action is necessary to achieve the objectives of the particular business.

Operations in Data Processing

Before production can be commenced in the factory, raw materials and parts have to be procured, which involves the data processing system in the preparation of purchase orders. When supplies are received, they have to be recorded on appropriate stock or job records, which again involve data processing. The accounts of suppliers have to be updated to show the value of the goods purchased from them and the remittances made to them.

When production is due to commence materials and parts have to be issued to the production centres and suitably recorded on issue notes which are subsequently recorded on stock and job records. The issues are often priced and extended, which are also data processing operations.

Factory employees are remunerated either for their attendance time, piecework or bonus earnings, and here the data processing system is concerned with wages calculation, preparation of payslips and the collection and summarisation of data with regard to production orders or jobs.

On completion of production, the goods are despatched to customers, which involves the data processing system in the preparation of despatch documentation, invoices, sales ledger updating and the preparation of statements of account. Eventually, remittances are received from customers, which involve further data processing in respect of adjustments to the balances on customers' accounts.

Jacob W. Chikuhwa

The results of business transactions (operations) for specific operating periods are summarised and presented to management in the form of operating reports, profit and loss statements and balance sheets.

The production of information from data involves data processing systems that comprise of those procedures, people and machines devoted to recording and manipulating raw data. Thus, data processing is a statistical art or science in which data are processed to produce information.

Data derive most directly from business activity. They are created in the many business transactions taking place daily. Besides, data arise from the environment in which a firm operates. Knowledge of environmental characteristics like incomes, taxes, tastes and habits help a business firm to recognise and profit from market demands; actions of competitors also provide valuable information for business managers.

Like in any manufacturing (processing) plant, data processing involves certain operations whose categories are divided into seven stages. These stages are similar in nature as the Basic Steps in Accounting Procedures discussed before (see page 47).

Nature of Business Data Processing

A business data processing system is an artificial man-made entity, which must be created, developed, implemented and managed. Like all managerial projects, it requires planning, organising, co-ordinating, controlling and staffing. The creation of a data processing system requires a combination of art, science, theory, principles, methods and practice.

A modern business firm cannot operate just by relying on past experience; it must undergo continual change and improvement in its operations. To operate such a firm without a flexible, quick response and efficient information system, which provides data on current operations and forecasts changing conditions, would be impossible.

The principal objectives of a typical manufacturing accounting system are the support of the following two major business functions:

    (i) Cost Control — all the costs involved, like labour, material inventory and transportation must be controlled and maintained at the lowest possible level.

Data Processing Concepts

(ii) Operational Control — to survive and remain competitive, a manufacturing firm must maintain an efficient and high-level utilisation of equipment, keep a well-planned production schedule, have quick inventory turnover, high space utilisation, prompt customer service, immediate elimination of obsolescent products and quick design of new products.

It is necessary to note that the accounting information system has a mechanical structure. The basis of the mechanical structure, as in all business data processing systems, is the concept of a file.

A file is a set of records relating to a specific business activity. An example of a file is the accounts receivable file. At a department store, for instance it is made up of the individual records for the credit (charge) customers of the store. Each individual record shows, basically the amount of money that a customer owes the store. Each record may also contain some or all of the following facts for a customer:

(i) Name and address

(ii) Credit standing or credit limit

(iii) Date of the last payment

(iv) Details on unpaid credit transactions (dates, items purchased, prices and costs, etc.)

(v) Customer's employers and monthly salary

The basic accounts receivable file just described is the master file of the accounts receivable system. Customer transactions (purchases or payments) are recorded in a transaction file and used to update the records in the master file. Other changes to the master file are recorded in a change file and made as well. Records for departing customers must be purged from the file (the records must be closed out and withdrawn from the file). Poor credit risks must also be purged. Customer records change as customers marry, lose family members in death, change address, change credit status, etc. It is clear then that a master file is created; then transactions and changes are recorded and used to change the master file to keep it current.

Obviously, various reports must be created by the system. Management must know the amount and rate of default (uncollectables) on credit sales. They must also know the volume of such sales in total and by department, etc. These reports are created from the transactions, the changes and the updated master file.

Jacob W. Chikuhwa

Management reports are developed from the flow of transactions and changes affecting the master file and from the updated master file itself. Like any system, a business data processing system is created and operated for a purpose. In other words, it is an organised endeavour with one or more definite objectives in mind. The reasons for capturing the facts associated with business transactions and processing them can be grouped in three general categories:

(i) Management Planning and Control Activities — management must plan for future activity and exercise control over current activity if plans are to be carried out successfully. Such actions determine the profitability (success) of the enterprise. If we are to take a department store as an example; the management of the department store must know if actual sales are below, equal to, or above expected sales. Inventory amounts (number of suits by size, colour and style) must be adjusted to actual sales. If, in another department of the store, fewer suits are being sold than anticipated, unsold suits will remain in stock. Prices (and profit margins) may have to be reduced in order to move the suits out to make room for faster-selling items. If sales are equal to expectations, then the suits purchased can all be sold, and future orders can continue at planned levels. In other words, the same plan of action can continue because it is successful.

Obviously, if actual sales are above expected sales, adjustments in plans are called for. The number of suits ordered has not satisfied customer demands; therefore; plans need to be modified and the pace of orders stepped up. It should even be that more salespersons, stock clerks and tailors are required to handle the increased sales.

(ii) Basis for Custodial (Maintenance) Processing — just as the buildings, furnishings and heating systems of an organisation must be taken care of, documents (sales slips, paycheques, purchase orders, receiving slips, tax reports, etc.) must be prepared and their contents recorded, manipulated and compared in order to carry on the daily business routine. Employees must be paid and customers must be billed. Purchase orders must be prepared to obtain supplies for the enterprise and supplier invoices must be recorded for payment as goods are received. Legal reporting requirements

Data Processing Concepts

(income tax reports, health reports on employees handling food, etc.) must be met if the enterprise is not to be forced to close down. Such activities are necessary to continued operation, although they may contribute only indirectly to profit (success).

Data generated by transactions and contained on custodial documents may serve as the basis for information reports to management; but the processing necessary to their production and use (completing a purchase order, for example), although required to keep the operation going, is not a basic planning or control activity of management.

(iii) Provision of Historical Facts — planning cannot be rational without historical data to use in establishing past and current trends and tendencies. Furthermore, adequate management control of any activity requires the recognition of performance standards. Such standards are most often obtained from the analysis of past (historical) behaviour. Legal requirements exist for retaining past data as a basis for tax and other reports.

The most important use of business data is in providing management with the information necessary to recognise trends and patterns in the activities of the enterprise and in the environment within which it operates. However, emphasis on management information does not really come at the expense of the other needs for data processing. A data processing system that collects and preserves the proper facts to provide adequate information for management planning and control will of necessity perform the custodial processing required to keep the enterprise in operation. Nevertheless, a system designed primarily for efficient custodial processing may not necessarily provide good management information. The custodial approach tends to put major emphasis on reducing the cost of inescapable processing activities. Putting management information needs first, emphasises the importance of considering profit motives when striving for improvement in data processing procedures.

The characteristics of an effective data processing system are the need for the system to be timely, pertinent, precise and accurate and economically feasible and efficient.

(i) A timely data processing system will capture current data and output current information. For example, the department store manager who receives an analysis of departmental sales for the previous quarter one

Jacob W. Chikuhwa

month after the close of that quarter is reacting to situations that may very well have changed dramatically since the quarter ended. Timely processing that reflects current conditions can help a manager perform his duties effective and efficient enough to be able to nip any problems in the bud. Ideally, data should be processed into information fast enough to provide adequate control of the physical operation that generated the data. In such a case, information is fed back in time to affect the situation from which the raw data were generated. Such a data processing system is called a real-time data processing system.

(ii) A pertinent data processing system will provide the proper information and do the proper custodial processing. In other words, it should have logical precise relevance to the matter at hand. A system for evaluating performance for the shoe department in our mythical department store should not be overly concerned with reporting the colour of each pair of shoes sold. It should, however, attempt to capture data concerning the extent to which customers found shoes in the colours they wanted i.e. the reasons why potential customers were not served. On the other hand, the manager of the shoe department need not receive personnel performance reports relating to the personnel in the clothing department.

(iii) The terms precise and accurate refer to two aspects of what people ordinarily think of as accuracy (correct values). A precise value, for our purpose, is correct within the limits of allowable error. For example, the manager of our department store does not need to know that total sales in the notions department this year were exactly $125 235.79; he would probably remember this figure as $125 000. For the manager's purpose, the $125 000 figure may be sufficiently precise, sufficiently close to the exact value. Just how precise and accurate management information has to be depends on how the information is to be used. For planning purposes, it is definitely important that information be accurate, but it does not have to be absolutely precise. In controlling detailed operations at the department level, however, information must be both very precise and very accurate.

(iv) To be economically feasible and efficient, a data processing system must do two things: (a) it must not place an excessive burden on the physical operation generating the data to be processed and (b) it must give the most information possible for the dollars expended. The latter statement implies that it would not be possible to change an efficient system to get more information without spending more money. The

Data Processing Concepts

former is more complex If processing costs are too high, the physical operation will eventually have to cease. However, just the fact that the returns from the physical operation are sufficient to cover the associated processing costs does not mean that the level of processing is appropriate.

Centralised vs. Distributed data Processing

Centralised Data Processing

When a business comprises only one factory or office as opposed to a group of factories or other business units, then a centralised data processing system would be appropriate. If a corporation has many branches, as more or less all large corporations are, a centralised data processing system may not be the best for the total situation. Even if the centralised data processing system utilises all the data processing resources most effectively, the combined resources of the corporation may not be used in the best possible manner.

If a computer is implemented for the purpose of centralised data processing, the way it is used requires careful consideration. Sometimes the computer may only be used for processing routine accounting applications such as payroll, sales ledger, stock control, purchase ledger, etc.

To obtain the maximum benefit, however, the computer should be used to aid management in problem-solving and decision-making by the use of quantitative application packages for linear programming, statistical stock control, production planning, net-work analysis, discounted cash flow, etc. When a computer is used for all the functions within the business, it is a centralised facility in the form of a data processing and information system.

The benefit to be derived from a centralised service may be summarised as follows:

(i) Economy of capital expenditure due to the high cost of computers through having only one computer for use by the group instead of several located in the various units.

(ii) If one large powerful computer is implemented, the resultant advantages are: increased speed of operation, storage capacity and processing capability.

Jacob W. Chikuhwa

(iii) Economy in computer operating costs due to the centralisation of systems analysts, programmers, computer operators and other data processing staff as compared with the level of costs that would be incurred if each unit in the group had its own computer on a decentralised basis, i.e. avoiding the duplication of resources.

(iv) Centralisation would also facilitate the standardisation of applications, but this would depend upon the extent of diversity in the dispersed operations regarding payroll and invoicing structures, etc.

While centralised data processing managers tend to neglect the human factor and the special personal needs of local users, there are economic factors that militate in its favour. The advantages also include economy for personnel, ease in enforcing standards, and security.

If the computer is also communications oriented, whereby all operating units are equipped with transmission terminals such as visual display units (VDUS) connected to the central computer, then basic data may be speedily transmitted back and printed on a local printer. This would reduce any time delay in receiving computer output through the post or messenger service. The possibility of an integrated management information system then becomes feasible, as data from dispersed units is speedily processed for local use and information becomes available at head office by means of the computer files for corporate planning.

Such a centralised computing service should be structured in the organisation at a level which enables the data processing manager to report to a higher level of management than the departmental level or functional level for which he is providing a service. This enables policy matters to be established at Board level, rather than at functional level, which establishes the use of the computer on a corporate strategic basis in order to optimise its use. If the data processing manager reports to the managing director, he is free from direct inter-functional conflict as problems are resolved at a higher level.

Distributed Data Processing

For a multi-location corporation with far-flung operations, decentralisation is inevitable, and so the issue of distributed data processing must always be raised.

Data Processing Concepts

Distributed data processing must not be confused with decentralised data processing, even though decentralisation is a feature of distributed data processing. Prior to the advent of the computer, different companies in a group may well have used their own data processing installation, i.e. a decentralised facility. The centralisation of data processing was the trend of the 1960s, but the tendency of the new millennium has been a reversal of this situation, largely due to the development of mini- and micro-computers. These computers cost much less than mainframes, which makes it a viable proposition to install them in departments and branches on a distributed data processing basis. This is the philosophy of providing computer power where it is most needed, instead of concentrating all processing in a single centralised computer system.

A distributed data processing network would be designed on the basis of a philosophy whereby small computers in dispersed operating units may be connected by a communications network to each other and also to a large, centrally-located mainframe. The mainframe may support a large database, which would allow information of a strategic nature to be retrieved on demand for corporate planning.

The mini- and micro-computers may be dedicated machines being used for a single main purpose and, in some instances, may be used as stand-alone processing systems when appropriate. This situation allows a high degree of autonomy at the local operating level which encourages motivation, flexibility and a greater acceptance of responsibility by the local management.

With the implementation of distributed data processing systems, it is of no consequence whether small computers are located in the same building as a mainframe computer or whether they are situated the other side of the oceans. Distributed data processing allows a business to select the level of processing autonomy in respect of depots, factories, warehouses or sales outlets and offices.

Distributed data processing also includes the use, on a decentralised basis, of intelligent terminals, i.e. terminals with processing capabilities which may be used locally for off-line operations or for on-line operations linked to a host computer.

Distributed data processing is located close to the user and responsibility is with local managers. Thus, there is pressure to become more tolerant and friendly to the user. In other words, distributed data

Jacob W. Chikuhwa

processing tends to be more responsive to the needs of users, more adaptable to change and more suitable to growth.

Concepts of a Database

A Database Management System (DBMS) is a set of computer programs that controls the creation, maintenance, and the use of a database. It allows organizations to place control of database development in the hands of data administrators (DBAs) and other specialists. This DBMS is a system of software package that helps the use of integrated collection of data records and files known as databases. It allows different user application programs to easily access the same database. A DBMS also provides the ability to logically present database information to users.

The accounting data files are set up to suit the preparation of financial accounts; the marketing data files, the preparation of production schedules and the monitoring of inventory levels. These files frequently contain duplicate data about customers, employees and products (see Fig. 3).

Fig. 3: Database Approach to File Structures — Integrated Files

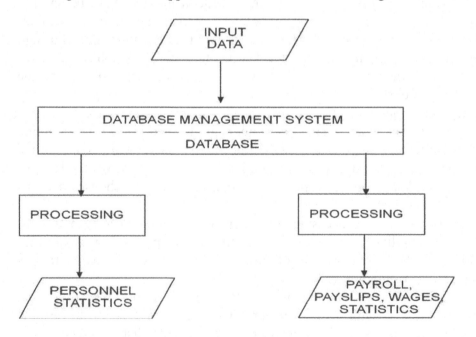

Data Processing Concepts

In contrast, the database concept requires the use of some form of general data storage. The organisation's data must be stored in such a way that the same data can be accessed by multiple users for varied applications. This can be accomplished by using a database, which groups, or structures, data elements to fit the information needs of an entire organisation rather than specially for one application or functional area (group). Thus, multiple departments can use the data, and duplication of files is avoided.

In addition to reducing redundancy and increasing data independence, the database increases efficiency. When a particular item is to be updated, the change needs to be made only once. There is no need for multiple updates as required with separate files. The integration of data also permits the results of updating to be available to the entire organisation at the same time. Furthermore, the database concept provides flexibility because the system can respond to information requests that previously may have had to bridge several departments' individual data files.

It is interesting to note that recently the use of prewritten application software packages has increased dramatically. This increase can be attributed largely to two factors: (a) the increased cost of developing application software and (b) the rise in popularity of micro-computers. For medium to large computers, the costs associated with developing and maintaining application software have become a very significant cost of doing business; one that can be reduced by purchasing prewritten software packages. The availability of these packages provides businesses and computer users with an alternative means of acquiring application software.

Computers and computerised record-keeping made it possible for the procedures and methods of recording and filing data to be converted from paper, file folders and file cabinets to computer software and storage devices. Computer access allows each department to maintain its own independent files. The personnel department would have access to the employee file, while the payroll department would have access to the payroll file.

88

Jacob W. Chikuhwa

Careers in Data Processing

The incidence of data processing in an organisation depends upon a number of factors, among which are the size of the business, the volume of data to be processed, the dispersion of operating units and the information needs of the various functions and departments of the business. In general, as volumes of data for processing increase, it becomes necessary to consider the introduction of a data processing department which would make use of mechanised or computerised methods of data processing.

Thus, data processing is a specialist activity consisting of different areas of technical specialisation. As with other departments, data processing departments' structures and staff compliments vary from company to company. The size of this department has a general relationship to the size of the company, but also reflects the complexity of the company's operations.

In broad terms, a largish data processing department is subdivided into systems, programming and operations. The dividing line between systems and programming is not quite clear and the two functions are sometimes merged into one.

It is also possible that systems is seen as a function outside the orbit of the data processing department, perhaps as a department in its own right or part of a management services function. Another possibility is where the system analysts are on the staff of user departments, either on a temporary basis or permanently. This arrangement has the advantage of keeping the systems analysts close to the actual work going on.

The continuing fluidity of the data processing scene has not yet allowed the careers of data processing staff to settle into formalised and qualification-based structures of other professions such as accountants.

APPENDIX

ORGANISATION CHARTS

The organisation charts selected for this Appendix are departments which are the entities organizations create to organize people, reporting relationships, and work in a way that best supports the accomplishment of the organization's goals and objectives.

Fig. 4: Human Resources Department

A forward thinking Human Resources Department is devoted to providing effective policies, procedures and people-friendly guidelines and support within companies. It is responsible for recruitment of professional and classified employees, benefits management, salary administration and job classification, training and development, records management, employee relations, and human resources information systems.

It also oversees organizational leadership and culture, and ensuring compliance with employment and labour laws. In circumstances where employees desire and are legally authorised to hold a collective bargaining agreement, the Human Resources Department will also serve as the company's primary liaison with the employees' representatives (usually a labour trade union).

Additionally, the human resource function serves to make sure that the company mission, vision, values or guiding principles, the company metrics and the factors that keep the company guided toward success are

Jacob W. Chikuhwa

optimized. The most common Human Resources jobs that are grouped in the Human Resource Department are shown in Figure 4.

Fig. 5: Accounting Department

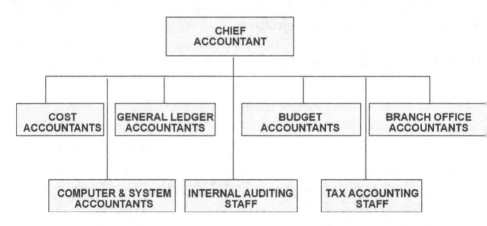

At its most fundamental, accounting is the development and communication of the financial and operational information necessary for management decisions in both the private and public sectors. The Accounting Department seeks to measure the results of an organization's economic activities and convey this information to management, investors, creditors, regulatory agencies, consumers, and employees. Core departmental posts are shown in Figure 5.

Under this broad definition, an Accounting Department would include audit, financial accounting, management accounting, and international accounting as special competencies in addition to the competency of computer technology-based accounting system.

Building effective finance functions is a key concern of organisations and finance professionals. Business partnering, business intelligence, benchmarking, outsourcing, talent management are just some of the solutions put forward to develop effective finance functions. It is believed that greater confidence in selecting the best course of action can only be achieved by carefully structuring and analysing finance functions and the unique contexts within which they operate.

Fig. 6: Finance Department

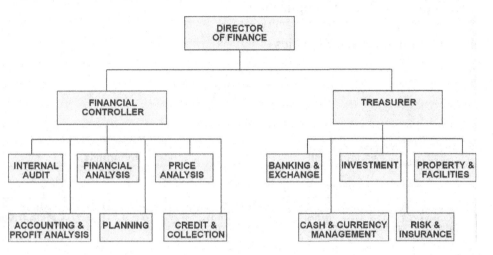

The framework of finance activities and the drivers that shape their implementation is shown in Figure 6. The main functions of the Finance Department include budget preparation, budget administration, cost allocation, accounts payable and receivable, banking and investment, technical assistance to service providers, contract administration and risk and insurance.

In other words, the Finance Department is there to ensure that there are adequate funds available to acquire the resources needed to help the organisation achieve its objectives; to ensure costs are controlled; to ensure adequate cash flow; to establish and control profitability levels. One of the major roles of the finance department is to identify appropriate financial information prior to communicating this information to managers and decision-makers, in order that they may make informed judgements and decisions. A Finance Department also prepares financial documents and final accounts for managers to use and for reporting purposes, e. g. at AGMs, etc.

Management has recognised that information is a scarce and valuable resource of the entire organisation and has increasingly emphasised the statistical data-processing activity and elevated it in the organisational structure. While economists and statisticians play a dominant role in the

Jacob W. Chikuhwa

department, its functions are now biased towards computer-based accounting and financial applications.

Fig. 7: Economics and Statistics

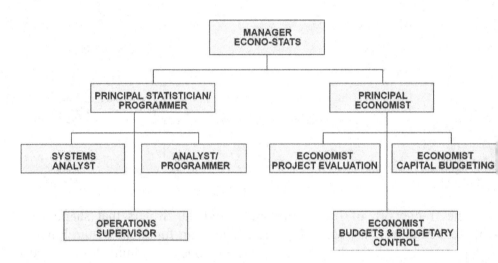

Whether designing new products, streamlining a production process or evaluating current vs. prospective customers, today's business managers face greater complexities than ever before. Running a grocery shop on instinct no longer suffices. Statistics provide managers with more confidence in dealing with uncertainty in spite of the flood of available data, enabling managers to more quickly make smarter decisions and provide more stable leadership to staff relying on them. On the other hand, the Economics Section is to provide economic analysis and studies to support a company in its operations and in the definition of its positioning, strategy and policy.

Therefore, the creation of an Econo-Stats Department should be accompanied by the elevation of its activity to the same status as the tradition line functions (production, marketing, finance, personnel). When it occupies this position, the department reflects a corporate-wide scope. The independent status of the Econo-Stats Department helps to ensure that each functional area gets impartial service and that their particular information requirements are integrated to meet organisation goals.

BIBLIOGRAPHY

Executive Guide to High-Impact Talent Management: Powerful Tools for Leveraging a Changing Workforce, The, by David DeLong and Steve Trautman, 2010.
Management, Tasks, Responsibilities, Practices, by Peter F. Drucker, 1975, LiberTryck, Stockholm.
Manpower Development Planning: Theory and an African Case Study (The Making of Modern Africa), by Berhanu Abegaz, 1994.
Organisation and Environment, by P. Lawrence, J. Lorsh, 1967, Homewood, Ill.
Thriving on Chaos, by T. Peters, 1991, Excel/A California Limited Partnership.

Accounting Flows: Income, Funds, and Cash, by R. K. Jeedicke, R. T. Sprouce, 1965, Prentice-Hall, Inc. Englewood, Cliffs, N. J.
Analysis and Interpretation of Financial Statements, by Professor J. Langhout, 1984, South African Universities Press, Cape Town.
Business Administration in South Africa, by O. Britzius, 1982, Juta & Company Limited, Cape Town.
Financial Management (Barron's Business Library) by Jae K. Shim Ph.D. and Joel G. Siegel Ph.D., 2008.
Financial Management: Principles and Applications (11th Edition), by Sheridan Titman, John D. Martin, and Arthur J. Keown, 2010.
Financial Management: Theory & Practice, by Eugene F. Brigham and Michael C. Ehrhardt, 2010.
Investment Decisions and Capital Costs, by J. T. S. Porterfield, 1965, Prentice-Hall, Inc. Englewood Cliffs, N. J.
Managerial Economics, by J. Dean, 1951, Prentice-Hall, Inc.

Business Data Systems, by H. D. Clifton, 1986, Prentice-Hall, International.
Computerised Book-keeping: An Accredited Textbook of the Institute of Certified Bookkeepers, by Dr. Peter Marshall, 2010.
Computers and Information Processing, by D. D. Spencer, 1985, Charles E. Merrill Publishing Company.
Concepts of Database Management, by Philip J. Pratt and Joseph J. Adamski, 2007.
Database Concepts (5th Edition) by David Krenke and David Auer, 2010.

INDEX

ABOUT THE AUTHOR

A national of Zimbabwe, JACOB WILSON CHIKUHWA holds degrees in economics and international relations from the Kiev Institute of National Economy in Ukraine, and the University of Stockholm in Sweden. He has worked as an economist and administrator in the public and private sectors for over 35 years and has lectured on economics, finance, management information systems and administration in Zimbabwe, Sweden and the USA.

Jacob Wilson Chikuhwa was born on 24th September, 1940 just one year after the outbreak of the Second World War. Being one of twin brothers, he almost became a victim of Shona religious belief. In those days it was considered taboo to give birth to twins. According to tradition, the younger twin was to be got rid of without delay. Jacob survived to go on to study at Hartzell Secondary School, Old Umtali (Mutare) Mission — an American Methodist institution established in 1898. After obtaining his Cambridge School Certificate, he briefly worked as a school teacher in 1963 and as a postmaster trainee in Salisbury (Harare) in 1964.

In August 1964, as a youth activist for a democratic Zimbabwe, Chikuhwa was arrested by the white minority Rhodesian Front regime. He was released from detention in 1965 and in 1966 he escaped into Zambia where he was able to secure an Afro-Asian scholarship to study economics in the former Soviet Union.

He graduated with an MSc (Economics) degree from the Kiev Institute of National Economy. Upon completion of his studies in 1972, Jacob Chikuhwa moved to Sweden. He enrolled at the University of Stockholm where he studied Economic Integration and International Relations. After completing his studies in 1975, Chikuhwa was appointed ZANU (Zimbabwe African National Union) publicity secretary in Scandinavia, West Germany and Austria. He was editor of ZANU's monthly journal in Scandinavia — *Zimbabwe Chimurenga, Impi yeNkululeko* (Zimbabwe Revolution). To supplement his party allowance, he got a job as an economist in the Swedish Postverkets Industrier in 1976.

Chikuhwa was able to return to Zimbabwe at independence in 1980. He worked in both the public and private sectors as a personnel and finance director until 1988. In 1989, he lectured in the Bachelor of Technology Programme at the Harare Polytechnic and at the end of that year, he went into voluntary exile in Sweden where he ended his career as a Bureau Director in the Swedish Postal Service Internal Audit in 1999. Because of his close contact with Zimbabwean liberation-movement nationalists dating back to his imprisonment and time in exile, Chikuhwa published his first book on Zimbabwe titled *Zimbabwe: the Rise to Nationhood* in 1998.

In September 1999, Jacob Chikuhwa returned to Zimbabwe as a consultant in collaboration with the United Nations International Organization for Migration (IOM). In April 2002, he once again went back to Sweden. He had a nine-month stint in the USA between 2005 and 2006 promoting his new book — *A Crisis of Governance: Zimbabwe.*

Jacob has turned to writing full-time. His works include *Zimbabwe at the Crossroads, Zimbabwe: Beyond a School Certificate, Shona Proverbs and Parables; In Communication with the Deceased; A Cheer for Sanity; A Handbook in Business Management.* He is currently working on an HIV/AIDS-awareness film script entitled *Venturing into the Unknown/Kumaziwandadzoka* and another title called *Sonnets of the Mind.*

Jacob Chikuhwa is married with two children; is a grandfather and lives in Stockholm with his wife.